CASINOS: ORGANIZATION AND CULTURE

CASINOS: ORGANIZATION AND CULTURE

PART OF THE CASINO MANAGEMENT ESSENTIALS SERIES

Chris Roberts

University of Massachusetts

Kathryn Hashimoto

East Carolina University

Prentice Hall

Boston   Columbus   Indianapolis   New York   San Francisco
Upper Saddle River   Amsterdam   Cape Town   Dubai   London
Madrid   Milan   Munich   Paris   Montreal   Toronto   Delhi   Mexico City
Sao Paulo   Sydney   Hong Kong   Seoul   Singapore   Taipei   Tokyo

Library of Congress Cataloging-in-Publication Data

Roberts, Chris.
  Casinos : organization and culture / Chris Roberts, Kathryn Hashimoto.
     p. cm. — (Casino management essentials series)
  Includes bibliographical references and index.
  ISBN-13: 978-0-13-174812-5 (alk. paper)
  ISBN-10: 0-13-174812-2 (alk. paper)
  1. Casinos.   2. Casinos–Management.   3. Casinos–Social aspects.   I. Hashimoto, Kathryn.   II. Title.

HV6711.R63 2010
795.068—dc22

2009007263

Editor in Chief: Vernon Anthony
Acquisitions Editor: William Lawrensen
Development Editor: Sharon Hughes, O'Donnell & Associates, LLC
Editorial Assistant: Lara Dimmick
Director of Marketing: David Gesell
Marketing Manager: Leigh Ann Sims
Marketing Assistant: Les Roberts
Production Manager: Kathy Sleys
Project Manager: Kris Roach
Full Service Project Manager: Yasmeen Neelofar
Creative Director: Jayne Conte
Cover Designer: Margaret Kenselaar
Cover Art/image/photo[s]: Getty Images, Inc.
Manager, Rights and Permissions: Zina Arabia
Manager, Visual Research: Beth Brenzel
Image Permission Coordinator: Kathy Gavilanes

Pearson Education Ltd.
Pearson Education Singapore Pte. Ltd.
Pearson Education Canada, Ltd.
Pearson Education—Japan

Pearson Education Australia Pty. Limited
Pearson Education North Asia Ltd.
Pearson Educación de Mexico, S.A. de C.V.
Pearson Education Malaysia Pte. Ltd.

Prentice Hall
is an imprint of

www.pearsonhighered.com

ISBN-13: 978-0-13-174812-5
ISBN-10:   0-13-174812-2

This work is dedicated to my family for their constant patience, support and encouragement. Without it, this book would be far from finished.

BRIEF CONTENTS

CONTENTS

PREFACE

The creation of any book is a labor of love and, at the same time, a humbling experience. This one is no exception. I've worked to share my knowledge and understanding about how casino resorts operate "behind the scenes" as well as in front of a customer. In writing from my personal knowledge and research experience, it forced me to closely and carefully examine what I knew and how I knew it. To improve it, I had many conversations with industry participants, regular gamblers, and other casino researchers. A few of these people have even contributed chapters in the book. I'm sure their efforts have helped to enrich the material.

This book came about through the genesis of a five-book series by a colleague of mine, Dr. Kathryn Hashimoto. Through her generosity, I was invited to write a book about the casino industry on a topic that I knew and was excited about. For me, that is the world inside the casino building.

Having initially worked extensively in the lodging and tourism industries, I quickly grew to love businesses that involve customers directly in the product. As with meals in restaurants and sleeping rooms in hotels, the customer consumes the gaming product as the casino provides it. The action is simultaneous and inseparable. That means the employee is just as deeply involved in the gaming action as the customer. That's exciting. That's fascinating. It's an honor and a privilege for the employee to be a part of the emotional experience of the customers.

This close relationship of employees and customers has led to the creation of a culture within casinos that is highly distinctive. More than other industries that I know about, the casino employee deals with the highs and lows that customers immediately experience at the gaming table and slot machines. It's not a meal that is purchased and eaten. It's a wager that may result in a win (cheers!) or a loss (boo!). With the meal, the customer always gets something. With gambling, that's never certain. This situation creates a tension, an expectation, and a wildness not seen in other businesses. The result is a cadre of employees who band together to commiserate about the customers, about the huge sums of money that flow through their fingers (but don't stick, of course), and a working environment of constantly being watched.

For the customer, the "luck" factor is very real. Some customers are very superstitious about which dealer's table they will sit, or which slot machine they will play, or even what clothing is worn. They often attribute wins and losses to the dealer, even though logically everyone knows the dealer has little to do with the outcome of table games. Slot players get "vibes" from specific machines, yet rationally they know it is just a machine. However, those feelings are real to the players and influence their actions. Capturing all of this is a goal of this book.

I've experienced so much of this myself. Given the prevalence of casinos in America today, I assume that the vast majority of readers have either played in a casino, or walked through one, or gambled at home with friends and family. I assume that readers will share my interest in this fascinating world. One doesn't have to gamble to in interested in the topic. Understanding it, especially if you are thinking of working in the business, is a primary goal of this book. I hope the book helps somewhat to give you these insights.

We thank the reviewers for their thoughtful comments. They are Priscilla Bloomquist, Ph.D., New Mexico State University; Dan Creed, Normandale Community College; Donna Faria, Johnson & Wales; Evelyn K. Green, The University of Southern Mississippi; Paul Howe, Morrisville University; Jayne Pearson, Manchester Community College; Jack Tucci, Missisippi State University; and Jim Wortman, University of Houston.

Chris Roberts

CASINOS: ORGANIZATION AND CULTURE

CHAPTER 1

AN INTRODUCTION TO CASINO ORGANIZATION AND CULTURE

DAVID C. WILLIAMS

Learning Objectives

1. To provide an overview of casino organization and culture
2. To learn the differences between organizational structures and culture
3. To understand the role of organizational structures in casinos
4. To understand the importance of casino culture to the casino business
5. To learn of the various leaders, including the "old-time casino boss" and the "big-name developer," who define casino culture
6. To be familiar with key topics that are discussed in upcoming chapters of this text

Chapter Outline

FIGURE 1.1   The Atlantis Resort and Casino in Paradise Island, Bahamas.
Source: Gunnar Kullenberg/Stock Connection.

INTRODUCTION

A colleague told me the story of his first day running casino operations for a well-established family-owned casino in northern Nevada The owner, and patriarch, was walking him across the casino floor describing how he built the business from a small slots house to a destination resort. As they left the casino floor, the owner said "unlike the corporations in town, we are a family business. I expect every one of my managers to be at home eating dinner with their families by 6 P.M. and be able to put their kids to bed." Having recently left a corporate-owned casino company, my friend was surprised, because he had come from a six-day-a-week workplace where late evenings were the norm. As the casino owner dropped the new executive off at his office, he finished with, "then we all meet back here at 9:30 P.M. to work the swing shift."

ORGANIZATIONAL STRUCTURES

As you embark on the study of organizational structure and culture of a casino resort, it is important to understand the difference between structure and culture (Figure 1.1). **Organizational structure**, sometimes called *organizational design*, looks at the tasks, relationships, and authority of an organization. Structure tells you how people coordinate work activities to produce results for the organization. I like to think of organizational structure like a human body. You have the skeleton that is made up of a variety of bones. Each bone is a position in the organization, and each bone performs a certain role. You can extend the metaphor to the muscles, veins, and major organs. So, from a structural perspective an organization is like a human body.

Organizational structure helps everyone in the organization understand who reports to whom and which department is responsible for which aspect of the business. If you need help with getting a room for a VIP player, organizational structure helps you know whom you should contact. Organizational structure ensures that responsibilities are delegated to the correct individual. Organizational structure shows how a decision in marketing should be communicated to the dealers, or hotel staff, or financial analysts.

ORGANIZATIONAL CULTURE

If organizational structure is the body, then organizational culture is the personality. **Organizational culture** is the shared values and norms that make an organization different from every other organization. Just as each person is an individual, each organization can be thought of as having a distinct persona. Culture helps every employee know what actions to take in a variety of circumstances. For instance, a culture focused on protecting casino games will have a Surveillance department working diligently to catch casino cheats. A culture focused on the high-end VIP customer will have access to a variety of amenities to ensure the customer experience exceeds anything the competition can come up with (Figure 1.2). Such a casino culture will also have a variety of executive casino hosts available at any time to meet the outlandish demands of a high-end player, sometimes called a "whale."

Many times the culture of an organization is driven by the chairman, CEO, owner, or central leader. While all employees play a role in developing the culture of an organization, the leader of the company plays a central role in establishing what the organization stands for. Actions taken by this leader tell everyone throughout the organization how they should act. If a casino boss is quick to bend the rules, expect the rest of the organization to act accordingly. If a casino boss is interested in the latest technologies, expect the organization to be filled with like-minded employees.

The history of the casino industry shows years of promotion from within and "old boy" networks. Movies like *Casino* suggest that the first casino operators in Las Vegas were

FIGURE 1.2 Venetian Hotel and Casino, Las Vegas, Nevada.

Source: Simon Harris/Robert Harding World Imagery.

FIGURE 1.3 The Luxor Hotel and Casino in Las Vegas, Nevada.

mobsters who moved from big cities in the east to find a place where they could ply their trade in the first legal casinos. Education in the casino industry started with learning the trade from the ground up. Dealers were promoted to supervisors, supervisors became pit bosses, and pit bosses became general managers. The long history of promotion from within created organizational cultures where the casino bosses surrounded themselves with like-minded managers whom they had personally trained.

Today the industry is filled with people from all walks of life and a variety of educational backgrounds. Casino culture has transformed into the organizational culture that you would expect in any large-scale customer service business (Figure 1.3). However, to understand the industry today, it is important to understand the history of the business.

LEADERS DEFINING CULTURE

In the gaming industry, organizational culture is driven by the leader or founder of the casino. This means that some pretty flamboyant characters drive the culture of leading casino organizations. Casino owners range from old-time casino bosses, to big-name developers, to billionaires who always wanted to own a casino (**the "gambler at heart"**), to Harvard professors, and industry **visionaries**. Whom you work for plays a critical role in how the organization operates. The casino boss establishes the values and norms that bring a persona to the casino organization. With a wide variety of casino owners comes a wide variety of casino cultures (Figure 1.4).

FIGURE 1.4   The Bellagio Las Vegas.

The Old-Time Casino Boss

Casino owners can fall victim to the same superstitions that players hold. Casino lore goes that a casino in northern Nevada had a craps table that wouldn't hold (make money). The table continued on a losing streak for years. The casino's owner tried everything. Each month the table lost money. Several teams of craps dealers were fired in his belief that the dealers were dumping the game and paying off cheaters. The owner moved the table several times and finally sold the table to another casino. That casino owner found that he couldn't win with the table either. Every month players would walk away with their pockets loaded with money. Again several teams of craps dealers lost their jobs in an effort to make a profit on this bad table. The legend ends with the casino owner taking a chain saw and sawing the table in half to ensure that it would never be able to lose money at another casino.

I always considered the story an urban legend. Then I moved to Reno, Nevada, to help renovate a closed casino. Before the major demolition started, a friend and I inventoried the entire property. In a storage room off an underground parking lot, I found something I'll never forget. Buried beneath a pile of old junk we found a craps table sawed in half. I can't help but think about the culture of that old closed casino. What was it like to work for a casino boss whose superstitions pushed him to saw a craps table in half?

The Big-Name Developer

Perhaps you will work for a New York developer and casino owner, someone with a famous temper and an unwavering ability to get the deal done. Being told "you're fired" on a reality television show is completely different from being told "you're fired" in the executive boardroom.

A friend who worked for a similar organization tells the story of the day the casino owner was viewing the progress of a remodeling project. A new hotel lobby was under construction and the owner wanted to see the progress. The conversation went something like this. "What the #$@% are you building here? The ceiling looks like %$#@! I will not have you ruin my resort with this type of work. What I want you to do is paint the ceiling black. Painting it black will tie everything together." Two weeks later the owner returned to see the progress. "What the $%#& is with the ceiling? Who the #%$$ paints a ceiling that color! Paint it white."

The Gambler at Heart

A friend worked for a midwestern casino owner with Las Vegas roots. The owner's father had built a casino in Vegas known for taking any bet. While other casinos put a limit on their action, this place would take any bet. The story goes that in the 1970s, a guy walked in with $250,000 and said he wanted to place the entire amount on black at the roulette table. In the 1970s that size of bet was unheard of. The pit boss called the casino manager, who called the owner. The owner said, "take the bet." The owner built a casino culture of being in the gambling business and building casinos that catered to gamblers. The other places could cater to families or big-name performers, but this casino was built for gamblers, by gamblers.

Over a few drinks my friend told me the story of the night he became one of the inner circle. He had been invited over to the casino owner's house for dinner, which was a significant honor. After dinner he and a couple of other managers were playing a game of billiards. The owner walked in mid-game and said "I'll bet you a thousand bucks you miss this shot." My friend shot back, "make it two grand and you're on." "Done," said the casino owner. The room went silent as my friend calmly sunk the last three balls to finish the game. The next words came from the owner, "damn, now that boy's a gambler." My friend held a variety of senior roles in this same organization over the next decade.

The Professor

Perhaps you will work for a former Harvard Business School professor. What would a former professor expect from his/her management team? In the book *Winner Takes All: Steve Wynn, Kerkorian, Gary Loveman, and the Race to Own Las Vegas*, Christina Binkley describes the central leaders in such a culture as **"propeller heads"** people who use data to develop strategic plans that other casino operators would consider folly. The culture of an organization builds on what the leader views as important. To understand the impact of leadership on organizational culture I think about a colleague who lived by the saying "what interests my boss, fascinates me."

Having worked in the Harrah's organization, I can tell you that the book *The Service Profit Chain* is considered required reading. The **service profit chain** describes a model of management that focuses on employee satisfaction, customer satisfaction, and their relationship to generating profits. Corporate leaders making presentations at the wide-flung properties across the United States used to offer $100 to any supervisor or frontline employee who could draw the service profit chain. After a few offers of $100 you would be surprised how many employees could draw the service profit chain from memory.

The Visionary

Other organizations are led by visionaries who built a reputation of accomplishing the impossible. In the book *Running Scared*, John L. Smith described an organizational leader who defied the odds to build a Las Vegas empire. Steve Wynn's vision for the Mirage

FIGURE 1.5   Manmade volcanic eruption outside the Mirage Hotel and Casino in Las Vegas, Nevada. Another casino, Treasure Island, is in the background.

Source: Image from BigStockPhoto.com.

(Figure 1.5) was viewed with skepticism by established Las Vegas casino companies, yet his vision changed the future of the Las Vegas Strip.

One of my favorite **Steve Wynn** stories comes from an alumnus of the University of Nevada, Las Vegas who graduated the year after the Mirage opened. His senior project was to determine how many days it would take the Mirage to close. The professor demonstrated that with the cost of development and the cost of operations the Mirage would need to earn $1 million a day to break even. Needless to say no one guessed that over two decades later the Mirage and its signature volcano would still be a centerpiece of the Vegas Strip. Organizational culture is built through vision. Steve Wynn offered a vision of the impossible and proved every naysayer wrong.

A colleague who opened the Wynn in Macau tells the story of Steve Wynn and his desire for perfection. Just before the property was to open, Steve Wynn decided to move a restaurant. This type of decision drives the construction team crazy, yet it spoke volumes to the Chinese population. By moving the restaurant at the last moment, Steve Wynn was saying "this is my place, and I will spare no expense to make it perfect for my guests."

KEY TOPICS IN UPCOMING CHAPTERS

Chapters 2–6 offer the reader insight to organizational structure in a casino resort. Because casinos operate 24 hours a day, 7 days a week, 365 days a year, they employ a large pool of labor. Small casinos employ 800 or more employees, while large Las Vegas resorts can have 8,000 or more employees. For the sake of comparison, in 2008, the $66-billion global organization Google had 10,000 employees worldwide. Coordinating the activities of 8,000 employees is a major undertaking for any leadership team. A well-defined organization and strong culture can help employees to know what steps to take when unexpected situations arise.

Casino resorts are typically run by a general manager who is responsible for all aspects of the operation. By understanding the relationship between organization design and organizational culture, the general manager can offer a great customer experience. The organizational design of a casino resort is built around the customer experience, and the organizational culture helps employees know how to best serve the guest.

Chapter 2 offers an overview of the entire casino resort. As larger casinos transformed into resorts, the power structure and the organizational design evolved. Today, many resorts are organized around operating departments such as casino, hotel, retail shopping, food and beverage (F&B), and entertainment. Critical back-of-the-house departments such as marketing, finance, and human resources round out the organizational design of a casino resort.

Chapter 3 explores the casino departments. Many casinos organize employees and management by types of casino games. You will find Slot departments, Table Games departments, poker, keno, bingo, and the race/sportsbook (Figure 1.6). Security and surveillance also fall in the area of casino operations; however, jurisdictional regulations may require these departments to report directly to the general manager.

Chapter 4 delves into the structure of hotel operations and the wide variety of departments needed to keep a large hotel functioning. Unlike stand-alone hotels, the casino hotel management team must work with the casino to optimize revenue from hotel guests and casino guests.

Chapter 5 takes the reader on a journey through the F&B departments. With restaurants to cater to every player's appetite, the same F&B team can be responsible for a five-star French restaurant, a buffet, and a series of food court kiosks.

Chapter 6 looks at entertainment, meeting and convention facilities, and retail operations. Some of the major activities that draw guests to the resort are discussed in this chapter. The many different types of entertainment, including lounge acts, large production entertainment extravaganzas, and concerts with famous headliners, are represented.

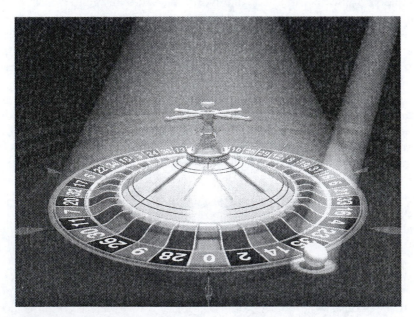

FIGURE 1.6   Spotlight on roulette.

Source: Image from BigStockPhoto.com

The role that the Meetings, Events, and Convention department plays in attracting customers is described. Finally, the expanded role that shopping now plays in the casino resort is explored.

Chapters 7–11 look at casino culture and the impact of the external environment on the casino culture. Casino resorts are built to attract and serve customers. As customers desire change, so will the design of casino organizations and the casino culture. Customer tastes, superstitions, and lifestyles all impact casino organization and culture. Larger cultural issues such as smoking, responsible gaming, and community relations all play a role in casino organization and culture.

As you will see throughout this textbook, there is no single best casino organization or casino culture. Different customers and different customer segments have different needs and desires. Each casino resort, each organization, and each culture has developed over the years to best meet the needs of its resort customers.

Conclusion

Organizational structure, sometimes called *organizational design*, looks at the tasks, relationships, and authority of an organization. Structure tells you how people coordinate work activities to produce results for the organization, and how to communicate. Think of organizational structure like a human body.

Organizational culture is the shared values and norms that make an organization different from every other organization. Just as each person is an individual, each organization can be thought of as having a distinct persona. Culture helps every employee know what actions to take in a variety of circumstances.

As you read each chapter of this text, think of the role organizational structure and organizational culture play in the modern casino resort. There are no right or wrong organizational structures, or no right or wrong organizational culture. Over the years each casino has developed a culture and structure that is designed to best meet the needs of a targeted customer base and its employees.

Key Words

Organizational structure 2	The visionary 4	The service profit chain 6
Organizational culture 3	Propeller heads 6	Steve Wynn 7
The "gambler at heart" 4		

Review Questions

1. Discuss the differences between organizational structures and culture.
2. Explain the role of organizational structures in casinos.
3. Detail the importance of casino culture to the casino business.
4. Detail the various leaders, including the "old-time casino boss" and the "big-name developer," who define casino culture.
5. Explain some of the key topics that will be discussed in upcoming chapters of this text.

CHAPTER 2

ORGANIZATIONAL STRUCTURE OF A FACILITY

CHRIS ROBERTS

Learning Objectives

1. To provide an overview of the organizational structure of a casino facility
2. To learn the divisions that support casino operations overall
3. To learn the functions of the back-of-the-house departments in a casino operation
4. To understand the function of the Accounting department
5. To understand the function of the Surveillance department
6. To understand the function of the Security department
7. To learn the operations of a larger casino resort
8. To learn of the function of the Entertainment department in larger casino resorts
9. To understand the function of decision making in larger casino resorts

Chapter Outline

Introduction
Slots and Tables
Back-of-the-House Departments
   Accounting Department
   Surveillance Department
   Security Department

The Larger Casino Resort
   Services
   Entertainment Department
Conclusion

INTRODUCTION

Most casinos organize their operations using a functional perspective; that is, the leadership structure is based upon the nature of the work to be done. Departments are created to reflect this work activity. The first department created is the casino itself. It is the heart and soul of the business. It is the primary revenue-producing department of the organization and has a large contingent of employees.

SLOTS AND TABLES

Growing from a need to support the casino operations overall, two primary departments or divisions are created within the casino: slots and table games. This division is natural for the business, as the Slot department primarily uses machines to offer gaming to customers. It has a relatively small staff to support and maintain the machines and to serve its customers. In contrast, the Table Games division has a large number of employees (dealers) who operate the many table games that are of interest to gamblers. Given this difference of slots focusing upon machines and table games focusing upon labor to deliver the gaming experience, it is natural to separate them.

BACK-OF-THE-HOUSE DEPARTMENTS

Supporting both primary departments are several "**back-of-the-house**" departments. These include the Accounting department (cashier's station, the countroom, and the bookkeepers), the Surveillance department, and the Security department. Figure 2.1 presents a simple organization chart for the basic casino operations.

Accounting Department

The Accounting department has three primary sections: the cashier's station, the countroom, and the bookkeeping group. The **cashier's station** or **cashier's window** provides services to gamblers, changing money into gaming chips (or checks as they are called in

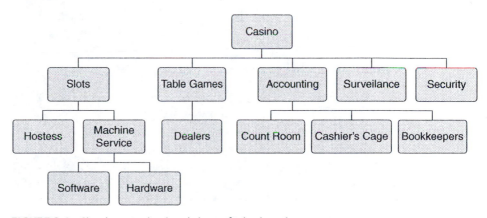

FIGURE 2.1 Simple organizational chart of a basic casino.

some casinos) so that customers can gamble at the table games. The staff also exchange paper dollar bills for coins for play in the slot machines. Today, most casinos offer regular customers, or those who join an internal frequent-gambler club, the ability to deposit money with the casino for use in slots gambling (Figure 2.2). Customers are given an electronic card that is similar in size to a credit card. The electronic card records the identity of the player and the amount of money deposited at the cashier's station. The card is slid into a slot designed for it on the face of the slot machine. The reader in the slot machine accurately tracks all bets and any winnings. The player can return to the cashier's station to redeem cash balances on the card at any time.

Of course, the cashier redeems the chips or coins that a customer wants to convert back to dollars when finished playing. The cashier's station has a large counter facing the customer side of the casino so the customer is separated from the actual money that is stored inside the station. This counter is similar to what you might find at a local bank. And similar to the concept of a teller window at a bank, the cashier station is often called the cashier's window because of this counter.

Because of the security provided to the cashier's station to protect the cash, chips, and employees from robbery and harm, the cashier station is often called the *cage* (Figure 2.3). This is because the security precautions often include placing metal bars across the customer side of the cashier's room. From the inside of the room, employees feel as if they are working inside a cage because of the bars that separate them from the customers. From outside, it also resembles a cage similar to what one might see at a local zoo. Thus, the cashier's station has the nickname of "**cage**." For more details on the operations of the cage, see *Casino Financial Controls: Tracking the Flow of Money*, in this series.

The **countroom** is a secure, windowless room where the money collected from all table games and slot machines is counted. Careful records are kept of the money received from each slot machine and table game. This information is tracked by shift so the casino

FIGURE 2.2 Advertisement for a casino's frequent-gambler club.

FIGURE 2.3 A casino cage.

management can identify how much money was earned by each machine or table game during any given shift of any day or night.

At each table game there is a metal box that is securely attached to the table, usually just under the rear lip of the table near where the dealer stands. It is locked at all times while on the casino floor. The metal box is marked with the table location and shift. There is a slot cut into the top of the metal box that lines up with a similar slot cut into the table-top. When dealers make change at the table, they slide all money collected into this slot in the table so the money drops into the metal box. Thus, casino industry jargon was developed that calls the money given to a dealer to wager at a table as the "**drop**," and the metal boxes are called "**drop boxes**." Slot machines also have unique boxes inside each machine. While the software tracks bets made using electronic cards issued by the casino, the slot box collects all of the coins put into the machine. The software operating the slot machines identifies the amount of coins that should be in a machine. This money put into slot machines is called the **slot drop**, and the boxes are also called *drop boxes*. The countroom team collects the drop boxes and carefully counts the money in the boxes. A detailed record is made of the quantity and type of money in the drop boxes.

Because of the high risk of transporting these drop boxes from the table games and slot machines, and to protect the integrity of the employees, a team of three workers is required to open the slot machines to collect the boxes. Similar teams of three employees are required to remove the drop boxes from the table games. To avoid collusion among employees to steal money from the drop boxes, the team of three employees must be from different departments. Usually the team consists of one person from the countroom staff, one person from the Security department, and one employee randomly selected from another department. In this manner, it is less likely the employees know one another and, therefore, less likely to make plans to steal any money.

The countroom employees are carefully selected for the Accounting department. Honesty is a prime requirement for the job. However, since the job involves counting money for hours and hours, the sheer volume of cash can become tempting to a number of employees who work in this room. To help protect the cash from theft, the employees who work in the countroom wear special clothing. Usually it is a one-piece jump suit that has no pockets, cuffs, or other folds of material where dollar bills or coins could be hidden. There are also rules and regulations on hairstyles, shoes, jewelry, and so on, that may be worn. These countroom workers are carefully searched at the start and end of each shift. They are also checked every time any of them enters or leaves the countroom for a break or meal. In this manner, the casino strives to reduce the temptation to steal, and to thwart any worker who attempts to steal.

This careful counting of the cash helps management make decisions about a wide range of business issues. For example, with this information, management can identify the slot machines that are used the most and look for patterns to learn why customers prefer those machines (Figure 2.4). It may be the location of the machines; or the particular style of machine; or the colors, pictures, and so on, on the machine. Similar information can be learned about activity at the table games.

Management can identify trends of business activity by observing the patterns of money produced by the individual slot machines and table games. This history is used to set expectations and to watch for deviations from those expectations. It is one method used to find threats to the security of particular games. When the volume of money produced by a machine or table game varies widely from its history, it helps to alert management about possible theft or other problems. All of this is possible because of the detailed records kept by the countroom.

The bookkeeping staff uses the information completed by the countroom and the cage to prepare daily reports of business activity. This data is combined with information provided by the slot machine software about gambling activity from the electronic cards

FIGURE 2.4   Slot banks at the New York-New York Hotel and Casino in Las Vegas, Nevada.

Source: Alan Keohane © Dorling Kindersley.

FIGURE 2.5 Roulette wheel at the Playboy Casino in Atlantic City, New Jersey.

Source: UPI/Corbis/Bettmann.

held by regular customers. Together, this information is used to create daily revenue statements (Figure 2.5).

Surveillance Department

The **Surveillance department** was created to protect and defend the guests, employees, and the casino games. It has the responsibility to safeguard the casino funds from both customers and employees. It is important to understand that the Surveillance department watches over people, the casino games and casino funds. The Security department is separate, but works hand in hand with surveillance since it has the responsibility to protect and police the entire casino resort property.

The Surveillance department watches all slot machine activity, all table games, and all transactions in the casino cage and countroom. Anywhere there is casino money, the Surveillance department has a responsibility to protect it. The primary method used is observation using very-high-resolution cameras. Advances in lenses and computers have led to the development of surveillance cameras that allow an operator to see very fine details on cards, finger nails, cuff links, and so on. The cameras are usually placed over every table game and bank of slot machines as well as all the public spaces. The operators in a secure back room can manipulate the cameras in a wide range of angles. A small dome is usually placed over each camera to protect it and to disguise the direction it is pointed at any given moment. Camera operators can turn the lens toward any subject of interest and can zoom in very closely, if needed. With the advent of digital recordings by computer, all images captured by the cameras are stored. If there is an issue, the images are easy to retrieve and review, frame by frame. Digital enhancement techniques can be used to enlarge any

FIGURE 2.6   Example of a surveillance central control room.

Source: Image from BigStockPhoto.com.

image to look for finer details, if necessary. Furthermore, facial recognition software can use these digital images to identify flagged players who are of special interest to the casino. They may be players with a past history with the casino, or players who have been asked to leave other casinos. Information on such players is shared by casinos.

If the Surveillance department identifies a situation where management should intervene, it alerts the casino floor management and the Security department. A team of managers is generally formed to approach players involved in anything of interest. Rarely does a single manager handle the case. The manager leading the team deals with the employee and customer (or customers). If the Surveillance department staff is needed to provide digital recordings, the manager handling the case will ask for them. The Surveillance department employees do not handle the customer or employee situation (Figure 2.6).

Security Department

The Security department is separate from the Surveillance department. The **Security department** has the responsibility to protect the physical assets of the casino. The assets include the buildings, equipment, and people. Whereas the Surveillance department uses observation as its primary operational method, the Security department uses a combination of visual observation by camera and staff who walk about the property to watch what is happening. They roam the halls, playing areas, and so on, to oversee the activity of people and any impact to property.

When employees require assistance to handle unruly customers, it is the security staff who respond first with management joining the situation as quickly as possible. Security handles any property loss. When something is damaged, or when patrons have a dispute (problem with betting conflicts, cars colliding in the parking lot, drunken and disorderly patrons, etc.), security handles the problem (Figure 2.7). The security staff is also the primary liaison with the local police department. Coordinating information and

FIGURE 2.7 Security agent patrolling the parking lot.

Source: Image from BigStockPhoto.com.

activity with management, the Security department leads the effort to protect the casino, its property, employees, and customers.

THE LARGER CASINO RESORT

Services provided to customers beyond the casino itself also play important roles in the organization. Figure 2.8 illustrates the major components of the organization and how they relate to one another. Key to this figure is the concept that the casino no longer exerts power over all other departments. In times past, the casino was the center of organizational

FIGURE 2.8 Typical casino resort organization map.

power within the firm. It called the shots and made the decisions about what other departments would do to serve selected customers. Today, the casino is still the number one revenue department for the business, but other departments are also important stakeholders. Given the rise in competition for the gaming customer, today the Marketing department is responsible for bringing customers into the casino. That role gives it strong organizational power. Rather than the casino manager having the decision power within the casino resort, it's the marketing manager who has the greatest influence.

Services

Historically, the casino was king of the organization, and the casino manager was the ultimate monarch. This was the standard method of operation through the late 1980s. What the casino manager decided was implemented without question by the entire organization. As gaming expanded throughout the United States, smaller operations began to question the need for all the "comps." They had a harder time making a profit especially when they were day-trip operations. For example, in Mississippi, casinos were approved to be the catalyst for recreational development on the Gulf Coast. The developers thought that casinos would be the major draw in the beginning but then they would create more recreation and entertainment venues to support the casino until people came to the region just to have fun. Because of this perspective, developers realized that while casinos were important, the hotels, restaurants, and entertainment venues needed to be more than just amenities. They had to be profit centers in their own right. Many comps were still offered, but it was no longer the main reason to attract guests.

Around the same time, Steve Wynn opened the Mirage Resort and Casino in 1989, and this perspective became more mainstream. Mr. Wynn announced that he didn't care which cash register was ringing in the casino resort as long as one was ringing. This meant that he had a new perspective for the industry. Rather than viewing the hotel, restaurants, and so on, as support functions for the casino, he felt they also should become profit centers. To help make this shift in thinking happen, Steve Wynn upgraded the restaurants to offer a better quality of food and he charged customers accordingly. Known brand names featuring celebrity chefs, such as Wolfgang Puck, were introduced. Wynn taught customers to expect better quality and to be willing to pay for it.

Hotel rooms that supported only the premium casino player were also viewed as a profit rather than loss centers. Instead, customers were offered larger, finer hotel rooms at a four-star level of service. Fewer customers were routinely and arbitrarily given free meals and hotel rooms. Frequent player systems tracked an individual customer's actual value to the casino, and awarded commensurate rewards. As a result, more hotel rooms were made available for sale at market rates rather than given away to marginal casino gamblers.

Entertainment Department

The Entertainment department also became an important revenue center. While some tickets are still given to premium gamblers, more seats are offered to customers at full price. Shows were reexamined for costs, impact, and effectiveness. Headliners such as Diana Ross, Madonna, were skipped over to bring in high-impact shows that didn't have such expensive star power. Extravaganzas were presented that had "wow" factors for the public but didn't have any well-known, highly expensive names. Other shows included groups such as Cirque du Soleil (a circus act) and Siegfried and Roy (a tiger show).

Retail shopping has also become an important revenue source. Instead of having small gift shops to offer daily newspapers, shaving creams, toothpaste, and other sundries, the shops today provide designer clothing, unusual gift items, and high-quality souvenirs. Many of the shops are contracted out to major brand name boutique companies. The concept is to attract players to the shops where they will spend winnings or use their frequent-player club points to redeem merchandise. As with the restaurants and hotels, the concept is to have customers spend money to generate profit for the casino resort as a whole.

In places like New Orleans where there were no hotels and minor F&B outlets in the casinos, comps became a difficult process. In order to offer the normal lodging comps, the casino had to contract with local hotels for a package rate. Therefore, instead of a simple line transfer from casino to hotel, actual money had to be paid out. Therefore, a hotel comp was more expensive. The same occurred with F&B. Yes, you could get a buffet at the casino, but if you wanted something better, the casino had to contract with outside restaurants. Again, this was a more expensive way to provide comps to loyal guests. In some cases, for these loyal, regular customers, trips to Vegas or other destinations were offered as incentives. However, the casino could afford only so many of these trips. As a result, cash comps were offered, but getting money back at the end of the night was not as big a draw. Therefore, what used to be amenity departments are now profit makers in their own right. While casinos are still the main draw to the resort, many people come for the other attractions.

Conclusion

As noted earlier in this chapter, key decisions are no longer the primary purview of the casino manager. Instead, the revenue-center managers have strong influence in decision making. The marketing manager has the greatest pressure to generate masses of visitors to the casino, to sell advance hotel rooms, and to sell seats to entertainment productions. When successful at doing this, the marketing executive has demonstrated effectiveness, which translates into authority within the organization. The rest of the departments defer to the marketing executive, as it is he/she who brings the customer into the facility—the customer who ultimately spends money on gambling, hotel rooms, meals, and/or entertainment. Each department, operating with this sense of profit generation, can exert its own authority to take actions to create revenues and increase shareholder wealth. This has helped to create a more level playing field in terms of the role and importance of each department within the larger casino resort.

Key Words

Back-of–the-house departments *11*

Cashier's station *11*

Cashier's window *11*

Cage *12*

Countroom *12*

Drop *13*

Drop box *13*

Slot drop *13*

Surveillance department *15*

Security department *16*

Review Questions

1. Explain the organizational structure of a casino facility.
2. List the divisions that support the overall casino operations.
3. Explain the function of the back-of-the-house departments in a casino operation.
4. Detail the functions of the Accounting department.
5. Detail the functions of the Surveillance department.
6. Detail the functions of the Security department.
7. Explain the operations of a larger casino resort.
8. Detail the functions of the Entertainment department in larger casino resorts.
9. Explain the function of decision making in larger casino resorts.

CHAPTER 3

CASINO DEPARTMENTS AND FUNCTIONS

CHRIS ROBERTS

Learning Objectives

1. To provide an overview of casino departments and functions
2. To learn of the importance of the design and placement of slots
3. To learn of the importance of job positions in the Slot department
4. To provide an overview of the Table Games department
5. To learn of the rules and importance of blackjack, roulette, craps, and baccarat to the Table Games department
6. To learn of the rules and importance of keno and poker to the Table Games department
7. To understand how currency is handled in casino operations
8. To provide an overview of the Security and Surveillance departments

Chapter Outline

INTRODUCTION

The successful operation of a casino involves many people and a number of departments. This chapter gives a brief summary. For a more in-depth discussion, read *Gaming Methods: Games, Probabilities, and Controls*, the games book of this series. At the head of the casino is the casino manager. The **casino manager** is responsible for all gaming activity within the casino. This person is carefully chosen for his/her knowledge of gaming, experience with running gaming operations, and ability to manage the organization's primary revenue source: the casino floor. This person's office is typically located in the **back-of-the-house**, where the support functions are located. These back-of-the-house departments include the accounting staff, the countroom and cage, and security and surveillance. While the back-of-the-house functions and staff are not visible to players, they play an important role in keeping the operations running smoothly. As a rule, customers are not permitted in the back-of-the-house.

As with many products and services in the hospitality industry, the delivery of the gambling experience happens with the customer playing an active role; that is, production and consumption happen simultaneously. We cannot store the gambling experience. Casinos, and hence employees, must be ready to deliver casino games when customers appear. Therefore, the casino floor is considered the heart of the business and is called the **front-of-the-house** as it is where customers play the casino games. Most of the customer interaction occurs in the front-of-the-house. Although casinos can have other divisions like bingo, racebook, and keno, most casino operations in the front-of-the-house have at least two primary divisions: slot machines and table games. Because the gambler is playing against machines in the Slot department, only small numbers of support staff are needed in that area. Dealers play a vital role in operating the table games. Given the stress of dealing, many dealers are required to operate a number of table games over a shift of eight hours along with many breaks to relax and break up their concentration. With supervision included, the Table Games division employs a large number of employees with a wide range of duties.

SLOT DEPARTMENT

The Slot department usually accounts for 60%–70% of the gaming revenues of a typical American casino, and uses much of the space of the casino. Foxwoods, the largest casino in the world, has approximately 7,000 slot machines! In contrast, casinos in Asia see only a small amount of slots play. Asian gamblers much prefer the table games. Thus, in Asia there are many more table games than slot machines. Customer gaming preferences vary by culture and geography.

In the American casino industry, income from slots creates the financial foundation. Typically, it is highly profitable. Most slot machines are now software-driven and computer-controlled. The payback rate can be set within the system using software commands. Casinos set the return rate. The **return rate** is the percentage of all money put into a slot machine, or wagered, that is then returned to customers. The **slot drop** is the industry jargon referring to all money gambled at that machine over a given period of time. Typically, this return range is between 93% and 97% although many casinos in highly competitive markets may set it above that. For example, at times a walk along the famous Las Vegas Strip, you can see some casinos advertising "99% Return" or even "100% Return!" The

99% return means the house retains 1% of the slot drop and returns the other 99% to gamblers. Of course, the 99% returned is not guaranteed to go to the same individual who wagered the money initially. It is just a commitment that of all money wagered at that slot machine, the casino retains 1% and the other 99% is returned to players. Given the random nature of who chooses to play at that particular slot machine and when, the money will be returned but it is unknown who will receive it as winnings.

With fewer moving parts, today's electronic slot machines perform better than the older mechanical ones and don't have to be serviced as often. Slot play is started by pressing a button on the slot console rather than by pulling the handle (which isn't even present on a large number of modern slot machines). To make it easy for players to gamble at the machines, there are several options for payment. Players today can use electronic cards (similar to credit cards in size although different in purpose) that have money credited to the card. It is similar to a debit card in a sense. Gamblers deposit money into their account, and then they can use the credit recorded on the card at slot machines to place bets. They place the card into a marked opening on the front of the machine. The slot machine then reads the card and displays the amount of credit for the gambler to use to place bets. Winnings can also be recorded on the player's card, thus reducing the time and effort needed by the customer when electing to stop playing at that machine.

In a similar fashion, machines can print out a slip of paper with the amount of credit you currently have, and you can use it just like the electronic cards. Players can also use coins or different denominations of bills to place bets at slot machines. By accepting the electronic cards and dollar bills in addition to coins, the need to make change for slot machine play has been reduced. With more durable machines running on software and more patrons using payment methods other than coins, the Slot department can operate with a small cadre of employees.

Design and Placement of Slots

Design and placement of slot machines is a key decision that highly impacts their use. The machines are arranged in a long row, typically 10–12 machines or more, to create a bank of slot machines (Figure 3.1). These **slot banks** of machines are lined up in parallel rows to create "avenues" of slot machines, similar to the bird's-eye look of a suburban neighborhood, to efficiently make use of space and to give the players a wide range of choices. Each slot machine has a stool or chair in front of it, so that players can sit or stand, as they might prefer.

The principle of the slot machine is essentially the same, although the actual configuration shown on the display screen of the machine will vary. The machines have three, four, or five spinning wheels inside, of which only a limited portion of the wheel is visible to the player. The object is to spin the wheels and have them line up in like combinations in the visible area of the screen when they stop spinning. Players enter a wager of some sort and hope for one of the many combinations. Payouts vary based upon the amount of money wagered and the particular combination that resulted.

Research and experience has shown that players are attracted to the bright lights, colorful machines, varied versions of games, and the sounds (and smells!) of the area. Most casinos place slot machines at or near the entrances to the casino and other high foot-traffic areas, making slots highly available for impulse play. Research indicates that heart rate is increased by red lights and loud noises, therefore slots immediately grab the entering

FIGURE 3.1   A bank of slot machines.
Source: Image from BigStockPhoto.com.

player's attention and create a desire to play. **Jackpots**, the larger payouts from any machine, attract the attention of other players, and act as an incentive for everyone. However, too much exposure to this high energy sometimes causes discomfort for players. Thus, the inner banks of slot machines generally use more muted, darker lighting and lower volume levels of machine activity. There is generally less foot-traffic in the center of the slot banks to distract players. This creates a more pleasing environment for long-term players. Jackpots, though, still generate extra lights and sounds so that other players (and management) are aware of the big wins.

Job Positions in the Slot Department

The positions needed in the Slot department typically include (1) the slot host, (2) the slot attendant, (3) the slot mechanic, (4) the slot computer system manager, (5) the slot shift supervisor, and (6) the slot department manager. The **slot host** has the primary function of providing customer service to the slot gambler. He/she walks an assigned area of the slot machines, watching for customers who are playing and who might want a beverage or some other form of support while gambling. Usually the beverages provided by the slot host are complimentary with the intent of encouraging gamblers to continue to play. Note that the vast majority of employees performing these duties are female.

The **slot attendant** has the primary function of maintaining the slot play area. If customers require assistance in the operation of a machine, the attendant provides it.

The attendant is typically assigned several banks of slots and then routinely keeps that slot play area clean and clear of trash, used drink glasses, and so on. If a machine in the assigned area needs servicing, the attendant contacts the slot control center to repair the machine. In summary, this employee is important to maintaining a welcoming, clean slot play environment.

The **slot mechanic** working today needs computer software and hardware knowledge in addition to mechanical ability. Given the vital role of slot income production, the swift repair of slot machines is a high priority. However, the security of each machine is a priority, too. The slot mechanic receives notice that service is needed from the slot attendant or the computer system manager in the slot control center. An employee from the Surveillance department joins the mechanic on the casino floor to open the machine. For security reasons, no employee is permitted to open a slot machine alone. The policy varies from casino to casino. Some casinos require at least two employees be present when a slot machine is opened. Other casinos may require at least three employees: typically one from the Security department, the slot mechanic, and the slot attendant. This mix of back-of-the-house and front-of-the-house employees, along with people from different departments, helps to prevent employee collusion. This group of employees remains at the slot machine the entire time the unit is open and under repair. It is only when the machine is again closed and locked that the employees in this small group can separate. Thus, the slot mechanic has primary responsibility for the proper functioning of each slot machine, but other employees always observe his/her service work.

The **slot computer system manager** supervises the computer system that operates the slot network. At the control center of the slot system, located in the back-of-the-house, this manager observes the performance of various banks of slot machines. Current slot usage is routinely compared to historical data as part of the analysis of usage. The manager uses this type of information to oversee the network. The manager watches for reports from the system that indicate a particular slot machine needs repair service or its coin box emptied, or a history of payouts. The software quickly identifies machines functioning outside of normal parameters. The system manager can then dispatch a slot mechanic to the troubled machine so that it can be quickly repaired and placed back into operation, or alert the slot shift supervisor if other issues emerge. Knowledge of computers and networks, software programs, and data analytical skills is needed for success in this position.

The **slot shift supervisor** focuses upon operations on the casino floor, including both the operation and usage of the machines; the employees who serve clients in the slots area; and the employees who operate mobile cash stations to make change for gamblers. The slot shift supervisor is responsible for ensuring that there is an appropriate level of service available to gamblers. This includes ensuring that the hosts are circulating regularly, providing patrons with appropriate complimentary beverages (liquor or soft drinks) and available to answer questions. The supervisor also ensures that slot attendants are circulating to keep the slot play area clean and attractive. During peak periods, the supervisor may have mobile cash stands brought onto the floor to increase the convenience of making change for gamblers. In addition to handling gamblers with problems (mechanical or personal), the supervisor is also responsible for managing the break and lunch periods of the hosts, and the cleanliness of the slots area. In some casinos, areas needing more than minor cleaning are reported to a separate janitorial staff while in others, the slot attendant handles these more major cleaning duties.

The slot shift supervisor is also responsible for the payout of larger machine wins, or jackpots. Usually, these are winnings in excess of a threshold, typically $50, although the threshold varies by casino policy. The rationale for requiring human intervention for larger wins has four primary facets. First, the slot machine may not contain sufficient coins at the moment of the win to repay the gambler. For instance, the machine may have been emptied recently and not built up a sufficient supply of coins to repay the entire amount of the win. Second, gamblers do not always appreciate receiving larger sums in coins. It may become too cumbersome for the gambler to handle so many coins at one time. Third, very large payouts (usually $10,000 and greater) are of interest to the Internal Revenue Service (IRS). An IRS agent usually wants to complete paperwork with the gambler regarding any large win. Finally, for protection of the slot games, the supervisor wants to be aware of larger payouts. Repeated large payouts to the same individual, or group of individuals, may signal a concern for management. The supervisor provides that general oversight through a vigilant awareness of the level of activity in the slots area. (Note that repeated large wins from the same slot machine are also of interest, but the slot system manager in the slot software control center should be alerted to this type of activity by the software, and coordinate with the shift supervisor and the Surveillance department to observe patron activity.) For these reasons, casinos like the cashless machines better. There are no coins or dollars, just computer printouts of winnings. The slot computer automatically keeps track of the information and sends it to the main computer for storage and analysis.

The **slot department manager** oversees the entire slots operation. The duties include forecasting activity levels on a shift basis for the coming day, week, month, and season of the year. The manager coordinates with the Marketing department to identify promotions that would likely stimulate slots play, and to make the appropriate adjustments in service staffing for the slot area. Personnel and player issues are brought to the manager's level in situations where the supervisors are unable to resolve problems.

The slot department manager participates in general senior management meetings and is responsible for representing the department in overall casino planning efforts. This may include the reorganization of the slots area to conform to other changes within the physical layout of the casino; discussions about the preference of one machine style to another and future purchasing decisions; the use of color, lighting, sound, and smell to attract patrons; and revenue planning. The manager is also responsible for setting and managing the department budgets for labor, training, maintenance, and the volume of complimentary beverages served. The slots department manager usually reports directly to the casino manager.

As described earlier, the Slot department is the major revenue-producing area for most casinos in the United States. Although simple in concept, it is a favorite of American gamblers—mostly female—and usually accounts for 60%–70% of gaming revenue. With the adoption of computer systems to manage the software-based machines, most casinos are able to operate this department in an efficient and effective manner with small service staffs, an appropriate level of complimentary beverages, and a highly trained maintenance staff.

TABLE GAMES DEPARTMENT

Although it usually generates less revenue than the Slot department, the Table Games department is complex and attracts the larger wagers in the casino. The table games typically include blackjack (21), roulette, craps, and baccarat. Of these games, blackjack is the most popular and the most easily understood. The table games are generally located further into the casino, well away from the entrances. Often, the banks of slot machines surround the table games area.

The table games require at least one dealer per table, so the number of employees who work in this area is greater than in the Slot department. A **dealer** is an employee who handles the playing cards and operates the table game. A **pit** is a collection of similar table games grouped together in a small circle, and is managed by a **pit boss**. It is called a pit because the tables face outward so that customers can walk around the pit to select a game to play, while the employees remain inside the circle to operate the games. The pit is the interior space that is used by the employees. Customers are forbidden from entering the pit. The pit boss manages all of the active table games in a certain pit, ensuring the smooth flow of dealers to the tables, the cash and chips on the respective tables, and the activities of the customers. A **shift supervisor** oversees all table games operating on a particular shift, and directly supervises the pit bosses. The shift supervisor reports directly to the casino manager.

Blackjack, Roulette, Craps, and Baccarat

Blackjack is the most popular table game because of its familiarity to gamblers. Simple in its design, players are comfortable with their understanding of the rules and how to make bets. If not known to a particular player, the rules are quickly learned and easily mastered. The objective of **blackjack** is to hold cards that add up to, but not exceed, 21. Each card is worth the face value of the card, with 10s and face cards all worth ten points. The Aces are worth either 1 or 11 points, at the option of the player.

The game is set up so that each player competes for the best hand against the dealer, not one another. Thus, many hands can be dealt at the same time and all hands are competing against the dealer's hand (the house). The hand closest to or equaling 21, without going over 21, wins the bet. If the count of the cards exceeds 21, that hand automatically loses.

The blackjack table is a semi-circle shape, with the dealer standing on the long, flat side and the curved portion facing outward for the players. Usually a table has positions for a maximum of six or seven players, although only one player is necessary to operate the game. Each customer position has a chair so that players can sit comfortably while playing. Players may enter and leave the game at any point, and may sit at any of the positions that are not in use by other players.

Dealing cards is physically repetitive so that it allows the dealers to concentrate on maintaining control over the chips and money and watching the players for cheating moves (Figure 3.2). This mental focus is difficult to maintain, so dealers typically work for one hour dealing cards, and then take a 20-minute break. A primary duty of the pit boss is to ensure that dealers are given their breaks on time and a replacement dealer is on hand to fill the vacating dealer's position. When the rested dealer returns from break, usually that dealer is placed at another table. This rotating of dealers to different tables helps to protect the game. Players are less likely to follow a dealer because he/she attributes "luck" to a particular dealer. Further, rotating dealers helps to limit any collusion or cheating between dealers and gamblers.

Roulette is a table game that has a distinct shape. It is longer than a blackjack table, rectangular, and has a large wheel at the left end (as viewed by the player). The

FIGURE 3.2   A blackjack dealer following company policy to determining winners and losers.

Source: Kevin Horan/Getty Images Inc.—Stone Allstock.

dealer stands behind the table, near the wheel. Players may stand anywhere along the front side of the table or the side opposite the wheel. No player may stand along the area by the wheel itself. Players typically do not sit on stools or chairs at this table (Figure 3.3).

In larger casinos, several roulette tables are used to form a pit. In other casinos, a roulette table may be added to a pit of blackjack tables. This game requires just one dealer, and as similar to dealers at blackjack tables, the dealer works for one hour and then takes a break for 20 minutes.

Craps is an exciting game for players. It is played at a very large table, more than twice the size of a roulette table, and similar in shape. The craps layout is similar on the left- and right-hand sides with a unique area in the middle for special high-probability bets. Players may stand along the front and two ends, but not the area behind the table. Only employees may be in that area. Also similar to roulette tables, several craps tables are grouped together either to form a pit, or a craps table is added to an existing blackjack pit.

Five employees are needed to operate the game, which greatly increases the labor cost. Two employees act as dealers, each handling the similar left- and right-hand sides of the layout standing behind the table to monitor the various bets. A **stickman** stands on the player side of the table, managing the dice that the players throw, calling out the rolled numbers and collecting the dice for the next roll. A **boxman** sits on the employee side of the table, between the two dealers. The boxman supervises the betting on the middle of the layout, overall activity of players, dealers, and the stickman. Finally, a supervisor wanders around the table, both front and back, to monitor customer and employee activity. This is needed because of the very high levels of excitement and activity. Anyone can place bets at the same time, which can result in mass confusion and in some casinos,

FIGURE 3.3 Gamblers play at a roulette wheel in a Las Vegas casino.

Source: Las Vegas Visitor Information Center.

chips, or money can play. Often the players have friends and associates with them as well, adding to the crowd. The supervisor aids the other employees by observing everything, looking for unusual and suspect behavior. Generally, the roving supervisor remains anonymous while observing.

Baccarat is a table game with very formal rules (Figure 3.4). You don't have to know how to play; just know that there are two basic bets: either on the player or on the banker. There is a tie bet but it is considered a sucker's bet as a rule. How much to bet and where to place that bet is the only decision you make. However, baccarat has the lowest house advantage of all the games in the casino. Baccarat pits are for high rollers and often the table is placed in a separate room or cordoned-off space. Employees who work in the area dress in formal attire and behave much more formally, too. Players are expected to respect this theme, and dress and behave in a similar fashion. The game requires only one dealer, but typically, two to three other employees are present to provide a high degree of service for the players.

To respond to growing customer interest, **mini-baccarat** has been introduced as a new trend in table games. It is essentially the same game as baccarat but offered on a more informal basis. Customers are welcome with all forms of dress and experience. Usually the mini-baccarat tables are grouped together in a separate play area or room, similar to the more formal baccarat game, but the public is welcome.

FIGURE 3.4 Baccarat table ready for use.

Source: Alan Keohane © Dorling Kindersley.

Keno and Poker

Keno can be played anywhere in the casino. It is essentially similar to a state lottery where numbers are randomly drawn from a box of numbers (Figure 3.5). Patrons have previously marked from 1 to 20 numbers on a form, forecasting which numbers will be drawn. The more numbers that are correctly selected, the higher the reward. Most casinos have a dedicated place for keno, which is typically a space with rows of chairs facing a central

FIGURE 3.5 Keno game in progress at the Circus Circus Hotel and Casino in Las Vegas, Nevada.

Source: Alan Keohane © Dorling Kindersley.

podium where the numbers are officially drawn and announced. However, players can be anywhere—in the restaurant, bar areas, or even your hotel room. A **keno runner** moves from place to place, collecting player bets for keno. Winners take their winning ticket to the keno station for verification and payout.

Poker is a very different type of game for the casino. While all of the other games are designed to play against the house, poker is designed for the players to compete against one another. Basically, casinos act as an objective manager of the game. They provide a place to play and a dealer. To earn revenue, the casinos can charge the players a "vig" on the winning pots. A **vig** or vigorish is a commission on winnings. When a pot is won, the house employee counts the pot, retains a vig for the house (usually 3%–10%), and pays the balance to the player. The amount of the vig is dependent upon house policies. The percentage should be high enough to justify the use of the floor space, employee time, and equipment for poker (tables, chairs, chips, etc.), yet low enough to attract players. However, other casinos simply charge by time or game. They expect that the poker players will gamble at other venues throughout the casino. Some "off shoots" of poker that use a table and compete against the house include pai gow poker and Caribbean stud Poker. These games are operated with one dealer and are also arranged in a pit formation.

CURRENCY

To provide service to customers, the casino operates a space called the **casino cage** that exchanges player cash into casino chips or the reverse when players are ready to stop playing for the day. The name *cage* has been given to this space because iron bars often protect it. The purpose of the bars is to effectively separate players from the cash and the employees who work in this area. Given the large amount of cash that is on hand in this area, it is necessary to protect it from robbery. Thus, only authorized employees of the Accounting department are permitted inside the cage.

The **Accounting department** includes the casino cage, countroom, and bookkeeping staff. The **countroom** is a very secure facility deep in the back of the casino where money is taken from the table games, slot machines, and cages to be counted. The casino cage bridges the front-of-the-house so that players can exchange cash for casino chips and the back-of-the-house where the countroom and the bookkeeping staff are located. It is literally accessible to customers on one side, and accessible to the bookkeeping and countroom staff on the other side.

The countroom employees are carefully selected for honesty and accuracy. They spend their work time counting paper bills (the **soft count**) and the coins (the **hard count**). Often machines are used to count both bills and coins, and the employees operate and oversee the machines. For instance, given that American bills are the same size yet of different value ($1, $5, $10, etc.), care must be taken to ensure the bills are properly separated. The coins are easier for machines to count and manage because of their different sizes (Figure 3.6).

In a ruling in 2007, the U.S. Supreme Court has ordered the government to vary the currency because of the needs of many disabled persons (principally the blind), changing the size, shape, and color of the different denominations. It found that the currency did not meet the law under the American with Disabilities Act. When such changes are implemented, different procedures and equipment will be needed for the cage, slot machines, and countroom. More details on these operations can be found in *Casino Financial Controls: Tracking the Flow of Money*, the casino financial controls book in this series.

FIGURE 3.6   Counting money accurately is the key function of the countroom.

Source: Image from BigStockPhoto.com.

SECURITY AND SURVEILLANCE

Security and Surveillance departments are vital to the operation of a casino. The **Security department** has the responsibility of protecting the physical assets and the patrons for the entire casino resort. The Security department staff operate just like a police force throughout the resort and they work with the local and state police when necessary. They patrol the facility and watch for problems or threats to the business, identify needed repairs, check safety equipment, and respond to calls for assistance from patrons and employees. Basically, they are the visible part of the operation and so act as friendly assistance to guests. Security works hand in hand with the Surveillance department. When there is trouble, security employees respond to the action whereas surveillance might spot the problem first.

Surveillance is affectionately known as the "eye in the sky." The department usually has its own entrance and many casinos do not allow surveillance to socialize with the other employees. The autonomy is necessary to help ensure the casino games are protected. It provides the "eyes in the sky" that monitors all areas of the casino. Located behind the casino floor, the Surveillance department is well protected from employees and guests. Access to this department is highly restricted to qualified employees who have been screened and who have the permission of top management. Since this group watches the gaming employees and players, it is important that the methods of observation are kept secure and secret. Even the majority of senior managers are not able to gain access to this work area.

Using advances in computer and communication technology, the surveillance room is equipped with state-of-the-art video monitors and computers that record the visual images received by the monitors. Very-high-resolution cameras are placed over every table game and in strategic points of the slot area. These cameras are capable of zooming in so close that fine details on coins are visible. The camera operator can control the zoom, and can move the camera around to access different angles, if necessary.

With the advent of storing data images on computer disks, casinos now retain the visual recordings from each table game for an extended period of time. This serves several purposes. The immediate benefit is that the surveillance crew can rewind and review the recordings when there is a question about player or employee activities. Also, in the advent of a player dispute, the surveillance recording can be quickly accessed to help resolve conflicts. Furthermore, the recordings are useful in the event of any legal proceedings that occur as a result of a dispute or conflict. The long-term benefit is that computers can be used to look for people's patterns of behavior. This type of analysis can help the surveillance staff identify potential problems and take steps to prepare for them. This enables them to observe players and employees unobtrusively.

The staff hired to work in this department are carefully selected and trained. Many are ex-cheats who have agreed to work for the casino to help catch other thieves. The training includes both advanced knowledge in video recordings and storage, plus an understanding of the threats to the casino games. Learning how to detect potential cheating, scams, and so on, is an art that few people understand and certainly is knowledge that the casino doesn't want easily spread to the general public. Because some unscrupulous players attempt to run scams at a number of casinos, many firms have agreed to share knowledge of people known to create trouble or steal. Thus, the Surveillance departments of many casinos coordinate their efforts in order to track potential problems. They inform one another of people with whom they have had trouble, or even suspect they might have troubles. This sharing of information helps the casino industry become aware of serious threats from individuals and coordinated groups. As one can imagine, this type of information is very sensitive so it is protected and used carefully. The Surveillance teams often also work closely with local law enforcement and provide appropriate information to help the police and the courts deal with criminals and criminal behavior (Figure 3.7).

FIGURE 3.7   The elegant interior of the Venetian Hotel and Casino in Las Vegas, Nevada, is under constant observation by the Security department.

Conclusion

The organization of the casino is separated into the front-of-the-house and the back-of-the-house. In the front-of-the-house, the slot machines and tables games are offered to the public. It is where dealers and gamblers come together to play the games and it forms the heart of the casino. The back-of-the-house is where the Security and Surveillance departments are located. In addition, the Accounting department is primarily located in the back, although the casino cage acts as the bridge between cash activity on the casino floor and cash activity in the countroom. Together, these departments form the key aspects of the casino and are required for it to operate effectively.

Key Words

Casino manager 22
Back-of-the-house 22
Front-of-the-house 22
Return rate 22
Slot drop 22
Slot banks 23
Jackpots 24
Slot host 24
Slot attendant 24
Slot mechanic 25
Slot computer system
    manager 25

Slot shift supervisor 25
Slot department manager 26
Dealer 27
Pit 27
Pit boss 27
Shift supervisor 27
Blackjack 27
Roulette 27
Craps 28
Stickman 28
Boxman 28
Baccarat 29

Mini-baccarat 29
Keno 30
Keno runner 31
Poker 31
Vig (or vigorish) 31
Casino Cage 31
Accounting department 31
Countroom 31
Soft count 31
Hard count 31
Security department 32

Review Questions

1. Detail an overview of casino departments and functions.
2. Discuss the importance of design and placement of slots.
3. Discuss the importance the of job positions in the Slot department.
4. Detail an overview of the Table Games department.
5. Explain the rules and importance of blackjack, roulette, craps, and baccarat to the table games department.
6. Explain the rules and importance of keno and poker to the Table Games department.
7. Discuss how currency is handled in casino operations.
8. Detail an overview of the Security and Surveillance departments.

CHAPTER 4

THE CASINO HOTEL

CHRIS ROBERTS

Learning Objectives

1. To provide an overview of the departments within a casino hotel
2. To learn the functions and duties of the front office areas such as the front desk, the bell staff, and reservations
3. To learn the function and duties of the administrative and infrastructure areas such as sales and marketing, housekeeping, and maintenance
4. To learn the functions and duties of the Security department
5. To provide an overview of the differences between standard hotels and casino hotels
6. To understand how casino size, hotel organizational power, and high-roller suites differ in standard hotels and casino hotels

Chapter Outline

INTRODUCTION

There are stand-alone casinos where people can come for the day. However, it is more profitable for the casino if guests can stay the night. This allows them to play longer. In addition, guests tend to bet where they are eating and sleeping. As a result, a large number of casinos have a hotel as either part of the resort or attached in some manner. The purpose of the hotel is to provide the casino customer with one-stop services all in one location, making gambling a convenience to the larger pool of gamblers who might want to visit the casino. Of the ten largest hotels in the world, nine are at casino resorts. Eight of them are located in Las Vegas, Nevada, and the other two are in Malaysia and Thailand.

Originally, casinos built hotels to target premium gamblers because these players wager larger sums of money and typically play for longer periods of time. Thus, they represent important revenue to the casino. Such players are designated as Very Important People, or **VIP**. They are extended complimentary services such as hotel rooms, food and beverages (F&B), entertainment productions, and so on. Since there are relatively few VIPs, it is easy for a casino to track them. Now with the use of computers, anyone can be tracked for their level of play and frequency. As a result, having a hotel is an easy reward for loyal guests and becomes an incentive for staying and playing longer.

At a casino hotel, your level of play directly results in a better room. They want to reward you for your loyalty and money spent. As a result, the amenities provided in the hotel room can be greater than those given to the typical hotel guest and may include items such as deluxe bathrobes and slippers, minibars stocked with complimentary snacks and beverages, daily shoe shine, free laundry and valet services, and so on. The beverages served in the restaurant or bar may use a high-quality alcohol. If you are a VIP customer, you are encouraged to visit the restaurant and order the top-tier menu items such as steak and lobster. The VIP is also frequently given favorable seating at entertainment productions. In summary, the VIP has such a high value to the casino because of the profits earned from this player's gambling that the provision of these complimentary services is considered well worth the cost. The goal is to keep this premium player happy with the casino and that he/she continues to gamble during this visit. The casino also wants the player to return to the casino to gamble again. Having the VIP sleeping in the casino hotel helps to keep that gambler satisfied and provides ready access to the casino floor.

DEPARTMENTS WITHIN A CASINO HOTEL

Casino hotel operations are structured similar to those of a standard hotel. There is a front office that has a front desk, a bell staff, and a reservations center (Figure 4.1). A sales and marketing department supports the advance booking of the hotel rooms and services. The back-of-the-house areas include housekeeping, maintenance, security, and room service. In many larger casino resorts, the F&B service is a separate department that typically serves the entire resort, including both the casino areas and the hotel. In smaller casino resorts, the F&B department is also part of the hotel operations.

Front Office Area

The **front office** has a **front desk** area that forms the communication nucleus of a hotel. It is where a guest's first interaction occurs and where he/she turns for assistance if necessary. The front desk also provides information to housekeeping about which rooms are in

FIGURE 4.1   The front desk in a casino hotel.

need of service, when guests are checking out, and which guests have VIP status (in a casino hotel, there are many VIPs). This information enables the Housekeeping department to plan its daily work activities. The front desk is the communication hub of the hotel as it is where both guests and employees turn for information.

The **bell staff** is focused upon providing support services to guests. The bellman, who could be a female or a male employee, helps arriving guests with luggage and provides an escort to a hotel room. The bellman also provides an orientation to hotel room services, pointing out where things are, how to operate each, and how to contact the front desk and/or bell staff for any issues that come up during the visit. The bell staff also provides assistance to the guest during the "check-out" process by handling requests for luggage portage or storage. In addition, this staff helps with package delivery like FedEx and responds to small requests as for assistance with shopping bags during the guest's stay.

The **reservations** staff handles requests from guests to book hotel rooms in advance. The general public can call the hotel directly to make reservations, or any number of travel agencies (either through online Web sites or through a local travel agency) that make reservations for individuals. Additionally, guests can use the Internet to make reservations directly with a casino hotel. The Reservations department has the responsibility to ensure that the hotel isn't overbooked; that is, that reservations are accepted only up to the capacity of the hotel. Once enough bookings have been received to fill the hotel on any given day, the Reservations department then closes the Web site and its internal system for that date so that no more bookings are accepted.

The Reservations department prepares the list of arriving guests for each day. This list is given to the front desk each morning so that the desk clerks can begin the process of assigning room types to individual requests. Since not all rooms are vacant each day (some guests stay many nights in a row), it takes a careful review of the available rooms to ensure

FIGURE 4.2 Woman relaxing in her comfortable hotel room.
Source: Shaun Egan/Getty Images Inc.—Stone Allstock.

each guest's request for a certain type of room is fulfilled. Working together, the reservations and front desk staffs ensure that guest requests are fulfilled (Figure 4.2).

Administrative and Infrastructure

The **sales and marketing** staffs have the primary responsibility to promote the hotel. However, in a casino hotel, this staff must coordinate their efforts with those of the casino sales and marketing staff. The hotel is a major tool for the casino to service the high-roller and premium players. Free or deeply discounted hotel rooms are awarded to these valuable gaming customers. Thus, the casino marketing staff develops plans that utilize the hotel rooms as part of a larger marketing campaign effort. The hotel marketing staff must develop plans that work to sell hotel rooms that do not conflict with the plans of the casino.

Housekeeping is the "manufacturing" department for the hotel (Figure 4.3). It has the responsibility of preparing all of the hotel rooms that are for sale each day. It also cleans the public areas of the hotel. This includes the hotel hallways, the lobby area, and the public restrooms. For the hotel rooms that are being vacated that morning, housekeeping works to "remanufacture" that room for the next guest. The room is thoroughly cleaned. Sheets and towels are replaced. The furniture is dusted and the carpets vacuumed. The bathroom is disinfected and the room amenities replenished. Once the room is completed, a supervisor comes in to inspect for quality assurance. The supervisor then notifies the front desk that the room is prepared for the next guest to arrive.

For the hotel rooms that have a guest staying over for another night, housekeeping services the room by providing clean sheets and fresh towels, and replaces any bathroom amenities that were used the night before (Figure 4.4). The staff do this in an unobtrusive

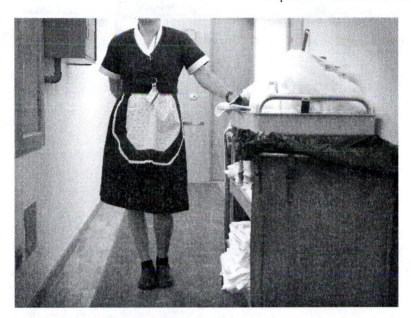

FIGURE 4.3   Hotel housekeeper in action.

Source: Image from BigStockPhoto.com.

manner as possible so as not to disturb the guest. Usually, the housekeeper enters the room later in the day in order to not bother the guest early in the morning. In some hotels, there is a door tag that can indicate "please clean the room now" or "do not disturb." Other upscale hotels have doorbells that can be de-activated when the guests are in the room thereby notifying housekeeping to come back later. In some upscale Asian hotels, the room is completely controlled by the room key card. When the card is inserted into its pocket by

FIGURE 4.4   Luxury marble bathroom with amenities.

the door, the electricity, air conditioning/heat, lights, and so on, are all activated. This saves money in utilities and also indicates availability of rooms for cleaning on a computer monitor. Most of the room cleaning happens between 8 A.M. and 5 P.M., although many hotels offer limited housekeeping service later into the evening, or in some cases all night.

Since some guests leave early in the morning, housekeeping targets these rooms first. Having some rooms clean and ready to rent early in the day helps the front desk assign these clean rooms to incoming guests who arrive early. Of course, some guests, who plan to depart the hotel room around noon or early afternoon, ask for a late checkout. Late departures are difficult for housekeeping for several reasons. First, as the day moves into the afternoon, more guests will be arriving and requesting to check into their assigned room. If guests from the previous night haven't left yet, the incoming guests have to wait until the room is vacated and cleaned. Second, the more guests that wait to depart later in the day means that housekeeping has an imbalance of work. In order to clean all of the rooms, the housekeepers need to work throughout the day. If too many guests wait until later in the afternoon to depart, then housekeeping will be faced with a larger number of rooms to clean in a shorter period of time.

In a casino hotel environment, gamblers often play late into the night, return to their rooms well after midnight, and often prefer to sleep later the next morning. Further, as hotel rooms are often a reward for the premium player, who doesn't pay anything for the room, this guest is not usually in a hurry to depart. The casino doesn't want this guest to leave, either. The longer this guest remains in the casino resort, the more likely this player will return to the casino floor to gamble some more. Thus, the housekeeping staff often operates with uncertainty about which guest is actually departing, and access to the rooms might be delayed. As a result, the registration desk at some casino hotels is located near a bank of slot machines so that guests waiting for a room can gamble. In cities like Las Vegas, you can check into your room and stow your luggage at the airport. In this way, if there is a delay in the readiness of the room, a guest can go immediately to the casino and begin playing without the problem of luggage. Then when the room is ready, he/she merely has to ask for the room key card at the front desk. The luggage is brought to the hotel from the airport and placed into the guest's room by the hotel staff.

Maintenance is an important support function for the hotel. With so many humans using the facilities, furniture and equipment have a high rate of use and require occasional repair. The maintenance staff provide this repair service. They fix water pipes, bathroom fixtures, electrical lights and power outlets, furniture, doors, and walls. They also care for the equipment and functioning of resort services such as the swimming pool and patio furniture, the hot tub, and any playground equipment for children. They handle the daily requests for repairs from guests, plus they work with the housekeeping staff to handle more complex cleaning and repair projects such as replacing worn carpets, beds, and other room furniture; repainting walls and trim; and maintaining room lighting fixtures.

Security helps the casino hotel protect its assets and the people who stay in the rooms and work in the facility. The security staff patrols the hotel on a regular basis by walking through the public areas, the hotel corridors, and the back-of-the house production areas. This helps the guests feel safe. The security staff keeps a watchful eye on hotel property. They help keep out unwanted visitors who might otherwise disturb the guests or hotel employees. Similar to the casino surveillance team, the Security department makes good use of cameras and monitors to observe the public areas of the casino hotel as well as the "back-of-the-house" areas where supplies and other hotel operations are underway. The cameras are never used to view into a hotel guest room. This combination of regular walking patrols around the hotel property and the use of cameras help this department keep an up-to-date perspective of the safety and security of the guests, employees, and hotel property.

Room service is a department that provides in-room meal service to hotel guests. Guests may call this department to order food items from menus available in the hotel room. The room service staff takes a guest's order, and then gives the request to the restaurant for preparation.

The kitchen of one of the casino restaurants typically prepares the food. The room service staff places the prepared food on a tray, adds any beverages that were ordered, and then adds other necessary items such as silverware, salt and pepper shakers, napkins, and so on. A member of the room service staff then delivers the tray to the guest room. Guests may charge the meal to their hotel account by signing the bill when the food is delivered to the room, or they may elect to pay the delivery person immediately. The bill (and any payment) is returned to the room service cashier for processing.

As the room service tray and dishes are not materials that are serviced by the Housekeeping department, the room service staff must return to retrieve the tray and used dishes. Some guests phone the Room Service department to alert the staff that the tray is ready for pick up once they have finished eating. Other guests either place the used tray in the hotel hallway, or leave it in their room for the staff to take care of the next day. If left in the room, the housekeeper cleaning the room places the tray in the hall and alerts the Room Service department to retrieve it. In order to retrieve trays left in hallways by guests, the room service staff makes regular patrols of hallways during slow periods, looking for these trays. The Security department may also inform the room service staff of trays it spots while patrolling the hotel corridors.

THE DIFFERENCE BETWEEN STANDARD HOTELS AND CASINO HOTELS

The hotel operates as any other lodging facility might, with one key exception: The hotel plays a key service role for the gaming customer. Using frequent-player systems, many of the guests in the hotel have complimentary or reduced rate rooms. Prized gaming customers are given free, and often upgraded, accommodations as a lure and in recognition of their value to the casino. Most of these gamblers are aware of their importance to the casino, and often demand a high level of free service from the hotel. A number of casinos use their hotels actively for these premium players. It is usual for a casino hotel to have full occupancy yet find that 40%–70% of the rooms are used as a "comp" or complimentary reward. One of the differences in a casino hotel and traditional hotel is that a casino hotel books only up to about a 90% of its capacity. As we saw in the beginning of the chapter, the hotel is a marketing tool to attract and keep guests in the casino. Therefore, it is important that an upscale room be available whenever a VIP or loyal gambler wishes to stay, even at the last minute. So, unlike a traditional hotel, the objective is not 100% occupancy. Thus, the hotel can be a revenue source for the casino resort, but it also acts as an amenity for loyal gamblers.

With so many premium players staying at the hotel, and with VIP services requiring extra resources, this places great pressure on the hotel staff to treat each guest with extraordinary care and respect—often without knowing the complete situation. Since the casino staff usually determines which gamblers receive complimentary hotel accommodations based upon the value of those players to the casino, the hotel staff may never know the true extent of each gambler's value. Any financial loss created by providing complimentary lodging and VIP amenities is an accounting line transfer to the casino Marketing department that extended the invitation to the player.

Historically, hotel rooms were considered pure amenities to the casino and the profitability of the hotel was never a consideration. However, as competition has increased, more casinos realize that so long as the guests spend money with them, it does not matter which place they want to spend it, casino or upscale hotel room or room service. Therefore, many casinos now view the hotel as a profit center where making money over their expenses is important. Casino comps are still important but their expense is balanced with hotel profitability.

Hotel Size

As a generality, hotels at casinos are larger in size, in both number of rooms and square footage of many rooms, than standard hotels. The primary reason for this is the need for the deeply discounted or complimentary hotel rooms given to the premium gambling customer. A second reason is to have sufficient lodging facilities that are convenient to the gaming floor. Having gamblers sleeping in the casino facilities helps somewhat to ensure those customers will spend some time gambling there as well. As mentioned earlier, nine of the ten largest hotels in the world are at casino resorts, primarily in Las Vegas. (see Table 4.1).

Hotel Organizational Power

Each department within an organization typically has an identified value to the firm, and therefore has some level of organizational power. **Organizational power** is the ability of a single department to influence the overall decisions made by the firm. In a casino resort, the Casino department has the greatest power. This is because it is the largest source of income to the organization. The primary reason customers come to the casino resort is to gamble, and this is where the majority of the profit is made.

TABLE 4.1   Ten Largest Hotels

Casino Resort	No. of Rooms	Location
1. Great World Hotel	6,228	Genting Highlands, Malaysia
2. MGM Grand	5,044	Las Vegas, NV
3. Mandalay Bay/The Hotel	4,752	Las Vegas, NV
4. Luxor Hotel Casino	4,408	Las Vegas, NV
5. Ambassador City (no casino)	4,210	Jomtien, Thailand
6. The Venetian	4,049	Las Vegas, NV
7. Excalibur	4,008	Las Vegas, NV
8. Bellagio	3,993	Las Vegas, NV
9. Circus Circus	3,774	Las Vegas, NV
10. Flamingo Las Vegas	3,565	Las Vegas, NV

Source: Executive Travel Magazine, 4-6-2008.[1]

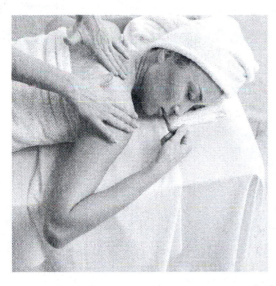

FIGURE 4.5   Woman enjoying a massage in the hotel spa.

Source: Getty Images—Stockbyte, Royalty Free.

In contrast, the casino hotel is usually not the central reason guests come to the casino resort. The hotel is viewed as a support tool used by the casino to reward its premium players. This makes it difficult when hotel managers switch from traditional hotels to casino hotels. Rooms managers typically wield power in a regular hotel because they control the revenue base. When they take a position in a casino hotel, their power is diminished because they must bow to the casino for room and pricing decisions. Therefore, it is important to understand this concept when making career moves.

While the hotel can be a profit center, with so many complimentary rooms given to premium players, it becomes more difficult for the hotel to generate a profit. The complimentary rooms do not generate income, yet VIP services must be given to the guest. Additional staffing is required in the casino hotel to provide the higher level of service demanded by these guests (Figure 4.5).

High-Roller Suites

Casino hotels have one area that is not duplicated in any other traditional hotels. That is because no other hotel has this very special category of premium gamblers know as **high rollers**. These gamblers wager very large sums of money and thus represent important profit opportunities for a casino. To reflect their value to the business, these players are given hotel suites rather than regular guest rooms. The suites are larger and are more luxuriously furnished. Some of these suites are known to be 10,000 square feet in size. Similar to large apartments, the suites have bedrooms that are separated from a living room. They can have five or six bedrooms, each with their own private bath. Some baths have ten showerheads so that you can just stand there and be drenched in water from all sides. Others have silver or white gold fixtures complete with trashcans made of similar materials. A dining room that seats ten with a kitchen complete with its own personal chef can be part of the suite. In addition, the living room with a fireplace, its own grand piano, and personal butler can complete the luxury. Finally, the top-of-the-line suites can never be

FIGURE 4.6   Attractive swimming pool area at a casino resort hotel.

Source: Image from BigStockPhoto.com.

rented. You cannot walk in and ask for these suites. In places like Las Vegas, you can only be "comped" these apartments and the price is a credit line in excess of $3 million!

These spacious suites are generally located on the upper floors of the hotel to give the high roller a good view of the outside landscape as well as to remove this player from the hustle and bustle of the regular guest areas of the hotel. In casinos that have a dedicated playing area for high rollers, special elevators may quickly transport the VIP from the special playing area to the suites. The idea is to make this high roller as comfortable as possible and to provide lavish attention, all with the intention of keeping the high roller in the casino. The longer this high roller stays at the casino resort, the more likely this player will gamble. The hotel suites play an important role in retaining this valued gambling customer (Figure 4.6).

Conclusion

The casino hotel is an important tool for the casino. It serves a few purposes. First, it provides nearby accommodations for a casino customer. This helps to retain the gambler by making it convenient to move from the hotel room to the casino floor. Second, the hotel rooms are used as a complimentary item for the premium gambler. It is both a reward for regular play and a lure to retain the premium gambler. Third, the hotel often has high-roller suites that are used to attract and retain the very wealthy gamblers. However, providing the complimentary lodgings and the higher level of service demanded by these important casino customers means the casino hotel has to incur higher operating costs. Complimentary hotel rooms do not generate revenue for the hotel, yet they have to be cleaned and serviced each day. Upgraded amenities for these valued customers are direct costs for the hotel. More employees have to be employed to provide the higher level of services. However, the entire purpose is to provide convenience and service to valued casino customers. The profit earned from their casino play outweighs the cost of providing the lodging and services.

Key Words

VIP *36*
Front office *36*
Front desk *36*
Bell staff *37*

Reservations *37*
Sales and marketing *38*
Housekeeping *38*
Maintenance *40*

Security *40*
Room service *41*
Organizational power *42*
High rollers *43*

Review Questions

1. Provide an overview of the departments within a casino hotel and discuss each.
2. Explain the functions and duties of the front office areas such as the front desk, the bell staff, and reservations.
3. Explain the function and duties of the administrative and infrastructure areas such as sales and marketing, housekeeping, and maintenance.
4. Explain the functions and duties of the Security department.
5. Discuss the role and function of services in a larger casino resort.
6. Discuss the role and function of the Entertainment department in a larger casino resort.
7. Detail some of the differences between standard hotels and casino hotels.
8. Explain how casino size, hotel organizational power, and high-roller suites differ in standard hotels and casino hotels.

Endnote

1. Executive Travel Magazine, 4-6-2008. Retrieved July 1, 2008, from http://www.executivetravelmagazine. com/page/World%27s+largest+hotels?t=anon.

CHAPTER 5

FOOD AND BEVERAGE

CHRIS ROBERTS

Learning Objectives

1. To provide an overview of food and beverage operations in casinos
2. To learn the factors involved in hosting a full-service restaurant in a casino operation
3. To learn the factors involved in hosting a buffet restaurant in a casino operation
4. To learn the factors involved in hosting a fine dining restaurant in a casino operation
5. To understand the differences between operating a regular restaurant versus a casino restaurant
6. To understand the factors involved in determining the quantity of food service outlets in a casino
7. To understand the importance of organizational power to casino food and beverage departments
8. To understand the importance of high-roller requests in casino food and beverage service
9. To learn recent trends in casino food and beverage service

Chapter Outline

Introduction
Full-Service Restaurants
Buffet Restaurants
Fine Dining Restaurants
Operating a Regular Restaurant versus
 a Casino Restaurant

Quantity of Food Service Outlets
Organizational Power
High-Roller Requests
Trends in Casino Food and Beverage
 Service
Conclusion

INTRODUCTION

Casinos usually have several food service outlets for the convenience of gamblers. In order to keep players in the casino, food and beverage are made available all the hours that the casino is open. The scope of food service usually runs the range of quick service, buffets, to full service and/or elite dining. The quick-service restaurants typically include coffee bars where beverages and small snacks are available to go or to consume at small tables nearby, sandwich shops, and dessert kiosks. Similar to a food court at a local mall, these quick-service outlets are generally grouped together so that people find a satisfying variety. Quite often, these food courts are on the fringe of several slot banks so that people can watch gamblers and hear the sounds of winning machines. However, as with all the operations selling food, the restaurant can be located near the casino floor but not on it. This is to allow minors, who cannot spend any time on the casino floor, to be able to eat with their parents at any of the food outlets. For example, in New Jersey, minors cannot step foot on any part of the casino floor, but they can usually walk around the outside and look in. On the other hand, Nevada law allows minors to walk through the casino so long as they do not stop along the way.

FULL-SERVICE RESTAURANTS

The **full-service restaurants** and cafés offer seated service and a little respite from the noisy casino floor (Figure 5.1). Usually, the full-service cafés and restaurants are colocated with the casino so that (1) the food service outlet is easy to access and (2) the casino is never far from a guest. Cafés and/or restaurants are often not walled off from the casino floor, creating an open ambiance so that dining patrons can observe the gambling on the casino floor and be reminded of what gambling opportunities lay there. These eateries offer full tableside service and have menus offering a wide range of traditional American

FIGURE 5.1 A dining room overlooking the casino floor.

fare, full bars for liquor service, or may be specialized by promoting a particular cuisine. Quite often, you can obtain a quick cup of coffee and a doughnut to go or a full sit-down breakfast at any time of the day or night. This is nice to know in case the coffee bar has a long line of people first thing in the morning or it is the middle of the night when the coffee bar is closed. The cafés are modestly priced and target families and the budget gambler. Many of the full-service cafés are open all night to accommodate the late-night gambler. The restaurants are higher in price and offer a more sophisticated range of menu items than the fast-food operations.

BUFFET RESTAURANTS

Similar to the full-service restaurants, many casinos also offer a different outlet that serves a buffet within the casino. Moderate in price, the buffet offers a family or group of friends a wide range of selections that appeal to a variety of tastes. Underlying the generous range of food items is the concept of speed; that is, the buffet offers food ready to eat. Because serving of the food is up to the eater, the speed of service can be as quick or slow as necessary. If a gambler wants to eat but does not want to take a lot of time from the gaming tables, speed is possible. Or, if a player has placed a cup on the seat or the coin slot of a slot machine, the player might be concerned some people walking by may not understand this is a "reserved" place. As a consequence, he/she may want to eat faster to get back to his/her "hot" machine. So, the gambler can enjoy a seated meal yet not take the time that an a la carte order from a full-service establishment would involve. Additionally, the food quality of a buffet is usually not as high as that of the full-service restaurants. The concept of a **buffet** is "all you can eat" so the restaurant attempts to control costs by using average cuts of meats (less steak and more chicken and turkey) or preparing less expensive dishes such as macaroni and cheese casseroles, garden salads, pastas, and so on. The buffets are often open for all three main meal times (breakfast, lunch, and dinner) but are not generally open all night.

Out of all the possible food venues, the buffet is used most often as a marketing tool to attract mass-market gamblers (Figure 5.2). One of the most common first comps players receive is the buffet. Because the buffets are already set up, costs are minimal, and volume turnover of the food keeps the food fresh, it is a low-priced ticket item given to players. In addition, because they are priced attractively to generate interest, these low-cost meals are intended to draw outside customers to the buffet with the hope that some will stay in the casino to gamble. To facilitate this, the buffet is typically deeper into the casino play areas than other food service outlets. Customers have to walk by many slot machine banks and table games before arriving at the buffet restaurant. Of course, upon finishing the meal and leaving, these customers have to walk by the casino play areas again. This double exposure to the casino play areas is intended to entice buffet customers to stay and play for a while. The goal is to cover the food and labor expenses of operating the buffet with increased gaming revenue.

Because the lines are usually long at prime dining hours, special lines are added for loyal, player's-club members. These lines have signs that specifically say that they are for player's club members of a certain order. First, this makes people who spend a lot of money at the casino feel very special and they are recognized for their efforts. And second, this says to the other people in the long line, "you too could be seated quickly if you spent a little more money." A kind of incentive, if you will, to remind people what benefits they could have if they came more often or spent additional money at the tables or slots (Figure 5.3).

FIGURE 5.2   The entrance to a very welcoming casino buffet.

FIGURE 5.3   Dining experience with an upscale table setting.

Source: Francesca Yorke © Dorling Kindersley.

FINE DINING RESTAURANTS

The largest casinos frequently offer **fine dining**, too. Starting in Las Vegas, historically, food was a cheap attraction. You could (and still can) have a $1.99 breakfast or a $3.99 dinner of prime rib at the buffet at some casinos. However, everyone knew that the quality was minimum, good, but cheap. However, when a casino wanted to attract an upscale clientele, it realized that high rollers ate and lived very well. They did not want to eat a cheap meal and they could afford and wanted to pay a higher price for a good quality meal. In addition, it was not just high rollers who wanted a decent meal, even many of the middle-ranked players would pay high prices for excellent meals. As restaurants became profit centers, managers realized that high-priced meals were great comps because the players felt more elite status walking into the best restaurant. However, even more importantly, players would pay for quality food. As a result, restaurants were outsourced to brand-name chefs and chains. Emeril, Commander's Palace, Charlie Trotters, Chinois, and Spago all tapped into the reputation of their creators and opened restaurants in casinos. The purpose of having these more expensive outlets is to attract the premium player as well as the gambler who prefers a lavish approach to the gaming experience. Many times a well-known chef is brought into the fine dining restaurant to help expand the menu, reputation, and identity of the restaurant. As with many fine dining restaurants, there is usually a formal dress code.

Part of the experience for guests is being seen as well as seeing who else is there. Since the fine dining restaurant is often the preferred choice of the well-to-do and premium players, some other patrons enjoy dining there just to be among such an elite group. This snob-appeal approach helps casinos cater to the premium player by creating a sense of importance about the fine dining experience.

OPERATING A REGULAR RESTAURANT VERSUS A CASINO RESTAURANT

The products and services offered in casino food and beverage outlets hardly differ from those of traditional restaurants. The objective in both instances is to feed hungry people, and food is food (even though it can be prepared in myriad ways). In casinos that cater to local populations, casino restaurants can be a draw for the meal crowd just like any other restaurant. However, the casino has an added bonus because a couple can go for dinner and then they can have a little entertainment beforehand while waiting for their turn to be called into dinner, or have an after-dinner amusement on the way out. On the other hand, casinos that cater to tourists (people who stay overnight) satisfy the need for food at meal times. Luckily, the guests don't have to go outside the casino resort for their food or activities. In that sense, the restaurants function just like any other resort operation.

However, the casino food and beverage restaurant can also play a different role. It is a tool used by management to help attract and retain the premium player, and to generate repeat gambling business for the casino. Thus, it is an amenity for the casino player. The premium player wants to be recognized by the casino for his/her value. Having the casino provide "free" meals is part of that desired recognition. The premium player often enjoys treating friends to meals in the restaurant in an effort to demonstrate his/her importance as a casino customer. The casino supports this thinking, encouraging premium players to gamble more by offering enticements of complimentary hotel rooms and meals in the various casino restaurants.

As an example, one of the largest casinos in America has a frequent gambler plan that is very simple, and thus easy for gamblers to understand. For each $80 wagered in either slots or table games, the player earns one point. The points are valued at $1 each and may be used in any of the casino outlets including hotels, restaurants, entertainment facilities, or gift shops. Given the relatively modest price of meals, the gambler can easily earn enough points to enjoy the meal services of many of the casino restaurants.

What is different about this restaurant guest is the sense of value created by the casino (Figure 5.4). By awarding the gambler complimentary meals and beverages in casino restaurants, the player often feels a sense of reward and importance. While not paying directly for the meal or drink, the player feels a sense of a VIP status and usually expects the food service outlet to both recognize his/her importance and provide the highest level of service possible to reflect that importance. To support this sense of VIP status for the premium players, the staff must behave accordingly, taking the extra time needed to fuss and fawn over these important guests. Undoubtedly, the player and his/her meal guests will order the finer selections from the menu, driving up food costs. Thus, the restaurant faces a situation of serving customers who are really there because of their status with the casino itself. Both labor and food costs of the restaurant are increased to meet the needs of the casino's preferred customer.

As we look at casino restaurants for locals versus tourists, we can identify some differences. In the locals' restaurant, patrons can come in for the food, just like any other restaurant. Therefore, being able to identify regulars, who develop a rapport with the wait staff, is important. However, in addition, regular locals will also be able to walk in and identify dealers and pit bosses by their first names so there can be a family feel to walking into a casino and its various food venues. On the other hand, regular relationships between customers and restaurant staff that might develop at a locals' restaurant rarely occur in a tourist casino restaurant. With the rapid turnover rate, it is more difficult to learn names since most repeat business is based upon the gambler's return to the casino. While the restaurant might offer an attractive menu with desirable food quality and preparation, it may not be the identity of the restaurant that matters to this frequent gambler. What might be more important is his/her ability to enjoy complimentary meals as a result of regular

FIGURE 5.4   Lobster dinner at the Royal Star Restaurant, The Venetian, Las Vegas, Nevada.

Source: Greg Ward © Rough Guides.

and strong levels of gaming play with slots or the table games in the casino, and be rewarded for it. As a result, brand-name chefs and restaurants are now part of the multiple food venues to attract visitors. The final difference between local and tourist casino food alternatives is that the local venues provide different specials and parties to create excitement so that locals will not be bored by the same menu. On the other hand, tourist casino resorts keep the same menus but increase the number of restaurants that are available at the resort. Therefore, people can go to any number of different restaurants for variety.

In summary, the casino restaurants must offer an interesting menu, provide high levels of table service, serve quality food, and be prepared to offer much of the food on a complimentary basis to the premium casino customers. Budgets must be built that cover the increased cost of labor for the higher levels of service and for the cost of food that is given away on a complimentary basis. Depending on the percentage of comps offered, some casino restaurants are often hard-pressed to reach the financial breakeven point. However, the casino management views this potential loss of profit in the food and beverage outlets as an important investment in retaining the premium gaming customer.

QUANTITY OF FOOD SERVICE OUTLETS

How may cafés, restaurants, and bars to operate is a management decision based upon expected volume of gamblers in the casino and the level of complimentary meals and drinks management intends to offer to premium players. The largest casinos often have 25–30 total food outlets, including quick-service kiosks, bars, buffets, cafés and restaurants, and fine dining establishments. Smaller casinos may offer a more limited range of four or five such outlets. With an objective of providing food and beverage service so that the gaming customer elects to stay in the casino and play, it is important to have enough food variety and seating capacity to serve them.

The operation of these many food service outlets could be expensive if each were designed to operate alone. Each would require a separate kitchen for cooking, and for storage of the raw foodstuffs. The nature of each menu would determine, in large part, how the kitchen is organized, and what equipment is of prime importance. For instance, if a kitchen staff were providing bakery goods such as muffins, bagels, and so on for a breakfast menu, then many ovens would be needed. In contrast, if the kitchen staff were preparing meals for full-service dining, then more steamers, fry cookers, grills, and so on would be needed. A duplication of equipment would also occur, as many cafés and restaurants use many of the same procedures when preparing common offerings.

To more effectively deal with these situations, usually a casino organizes the food service outlets in a way that enables the casino to have one master kitchen with perhaps smaller, specialized areas attached. This master kitchen approach takes advantage of the economy of scale concept. The equipment for the kitchen can be used for a wide range of menu items and at different times of day. Those food service outlets open all night can continue to offer full menus because of access to the regular stocks of the main kitchen. Purchasing of food is enhanced through bulk buying from food vendors. Storage is made more efficient by combining the needed stocks of each food service outlet into one master storage area, eliminating the need for separate storage facilities in each food outlet. Security of the food stock is also enhanced, as there is only one major location to monitor. Finally, room service for the hotel guests (the delivery of food to guest hotel rooms) is handled by this central kitchen because of its ability to fulfill menu items at any and all hours.

The Banqueting and Catering department relies upon this same central kitchen to prepare meals for the conferences, special events, and other functions held in the meeting rooms. Banquets and Catering allow customers to order special food in the quantities they want for a special party or event at the time and location of their choosing. Using the same operational design, purchasing, and food processing, the kitchen is able to prepare large quantities of meals and desserts for all of the function rooms. Planning in advance is key to success though, so that the kitchen can order sufficient food stock for the meals desired and have enough servers on hand to deliver the food in a timely manner.

To facilitate the operations of each food service outlet with the master kitchen, the food service outlets are usually grouped together in a row or circle around part of the casino area. From the casino side, customers can easily find the food service outlets and select the one they desire. From the kitchen side, having the restaurants in a row or circle enables servers to move quickly in and out of the kitchen area with customer orders. The same kitchen staff can prepare meals for a number of different outlets, reducing the number of workers needed. The service staff can quickly reach buffet tables so that food selections can be swiftly replaced as needed. The master kitchen concept, although complex and often busy, efficiently utilizes food stocks, storage capacity, cooking process, and staff to service the various casino cafés and restaurants.

ORGANIZATIONAL POWER

In casinos that still value comps over profit centers, food service outlets struggle to make profits for the casino. Given their role in providing complimentary meals for gamblers while using quality food stock and higher levels of service delivery, restaurant expenses are often a drain on overall casino profits. Restaurants become cost centers rather than revenue centers. Many modern casinos are working to alter that dynamic so that the food service outlets generate profits, but that is a difficult effort that is only slowly paying dividends in some cases. It used to be that comps could be as much as 90% of the dining option. However, now with the modern perception that restaurants should be profit centers, comps are more carefully screened and monitored for overall profitability to the casino as a whole.

The **organizational power** of the food service operations is fairly low in contrast to the casino floor. Many restaurant customers frequent the casino's food service outlets because they are visiting the casino. Although recognized as a needed function in the casino business, the restaurants and their workers are valued less than the casino. The casino hotel relies upon the food service operation to fulfill room service requests for the guest rooms, but the hotel views this as one of many services the hotel must provide to guests. The amount of time a guest spends in a hotel is much more than the time a guest spends in a restaurant. Even though the food service operation reaches more customers than does the hotel, the amount of money spent by the guest in the hotel is greater on a per transaction basis. Thus, the hotel views its role as more vital than that of the food service operation when it comes to satisfying its guests—especially the premium gamblers. However, in casino hotels that cater more to local guests, restaurants can be a draw as people decide where they would like to go out for dinner.

HIGH-ROLLER REQUESTS

The high-roller gamblers of the casino require additional food service attention. While the full-service restaurants cater to many of the premium players, the true high rollers of the casino (those gaming customers identified as the casino's most valuable) demand services beyond those available to the general public. These services could include unique menu offerings, fulfilling special meal requests, or hiring the services of a master chef. High rollers often want privacy in the casino play area, in lodging, and for meal service. In addition to requests for delicacies, unusual food items, and experienced chefs to prepare all, the high rollers often want to dine in elegant settings that are exclusively for them. They want to be able to invite special guests to share in this largesse. The casino needs to have such private and fancy dining rooms to accommodate high rollers. These exclusive rooms need to be located for easy access by the high rollers yet close enough to the kitchen so that the range of supplies and the cooking skills needed are at hand. The food needs to arrive in a timely fashion and at the correct temperature. If the kitchen is too far from the private dining accommodations for the high rollers, there is a danger the food will not be served in the manner in which it was intended (hot foods hot and cold foods cold).

Specialized hostesses are trained to serve high rollers. The sense of service is to be complete and seamless yet not be seen. Thus, the food service staff who interact with high rollers must be very well trained in the various cuisines of the world that are available in the central kitchen, the multiple methods of preparation, and the showmanship of seamless yet artful delivery of the food products. The casino's goal regarding the high roller is to satisfy his/her every food desire in an effort to retain the player in the casino. Of course, the "whales" (the worldwide top gamblers) do require very expensive wines and food, but this is only in keeping with their regular lifestyle. When a whale requests a bottle of Dom Pérignon (at least $150 per bottle), a special marketing employee, called a casino host, will immediately acquire a bottle or more. Some high-roller suites include a gourmet chef to cook as part of the suite services so that the guest is not inconvenienced in any way (Figure 5.5).

FIGURE 5.5 Hungry diner anticipating a meal of generous portions.

TRENDS IN CASINO FOOD AND BEVERAGE SERVICE

Steve Wynn's statement in the early 1990s certainly influenced the position of food and beverage in the casino. His focus upon having any cash register in the casino ringing up sales, not just those in the casino itself, fueled this shift. The casino interest has shifted from using food and beverage as a cheap lure to attract gamblers. This interest is now on generating increases in both food quality and menu selection, along with accompanying increases in price. Casinos have begun to offer inexpensive food courts up through and including fine dining experiences. While casinos continue to attract and retain premium players with a variety of food options, the focus has shifted to making the food outlets actual profit centers rather than just service centers. To move in this direction, some casinos are inviting name-brand restaurants to replace in-house restaurants. Some of the known brands are very upscale such as Bouchon, the Delmonico Steakhouse, Il Mulino New York, Spago, and Emeril's New Orleans Fish House. These restaurants typically price their meals in the $50–$100 per person range and often are in locations with commanding views of the Las Vegas Strip.

As mentioned earlier, many casinos are abandoning the use of cheaply priced meals as a lure for the casino, and instead are offering high-quality meals at reasonable prices. The intent is to use the dining experience as part of the overall casino experience, adding value for the customer by creating a memorable dining experience.

More structured frequent gambler programs help customers to understand what level of play is needed for them to earn complimentary meals and hotel rooms. This trend enables a customer to learn how he/she is valued by the casino, and what he/she can specifically do to earn a complimentary. This removes the guesswork by the casino employee about when to offer a complimentary to a perceived valued gambler. It also removes the mystery to the gambler about behavior that is valued by the casino. For many gaming customers, earning the complimentary meals and hotel rooms is a measure of his/her success as a gambler.

The trend of having structured frequent gambler programs also helps the food service operation anticipate the quantity of complimentary meals to prepare. The structured program can track the points used by gamblers for meals. Forecasting can be done based upon these recent and historical trends. Watching the patterns of what type of complimentary meals are requested by program members and when they are made helps management anticipate future requests. This anticipation of use can be planned for by ordering sufficient food stock in advance and staffing appropriately for busy periods. The records of the structured programs are invaluable for generating this type of useful information.

Conclusion

In conclusion, the casino food service operation provides a vital service. It prepares thousands of meals daily for the mass-market customers. It helps to cater to the premium players who desire higher-level dining experiences, and it supports the recognition system of valued casino players through the offering of complimentary meals and beverages. The food service operation is also a critical aspect of attracting and retaining the high rollers through its responses to their unique and individual demands. It also supports the Banqueting and Catering department in the production of food for functions happening in the meeting rooms. Although it is a challenging environment to be a service support for some customers (premium players and high rollers) and a revenue center for others (the mass market along with banqueting and catering), the food service operation plays a vital role in the daily operations of the casino resort.

Key Words

Full-service restaurants *47*
Buffets *48*

Fine dining *50*

Organizational power *53*

Review Questions

1. Detail an overview of food and beverage operations in casinos.
2. Explain the factors involved in hosting a full-service restaurant in a casino operation.
3. Explain the factors involved in hosting a buffet restaurant in a casino operation.
4. Explain the factors involved in hosting a fine dining restaurant in a casino operation.
5. Discuss the differences between operating a regular restaurant versus a casino restaurant.
6. Discuss the factors involved in determining the quantity of food service outlets in a casino.
7. Detail the importance of organizational power to casino Food and Beverage departments.
8. Detail the importance of high-roller requests in casino food and beverage service.
9. Discuss recent trends in casino food and beverage service.

CHAPTER 6

MEETINGS, CONVENTIONS, AND ENTERTAINMENT

CHRIS ROBERTS

Learning Objectives

1. To provide an overview of meeting and convention facilities and entertainment as part of the gaming industry
2. To learn the qualities and features of meeting room facilities
3. To learn the qualities and features of convention facilities
4. To learn the qualities and features of arcades and lounges and their contributions to casino operations
5. To learn the qualities and features of headliners and major attractions and their contributions to casino operations
6. To understand how retail shopping contributes to casino operations
7. To provide an overview of operations support

Chapter Outline

Introduction
Meeting and Convention Facilities
   Meeting Room Facilities
   Convention Facilities
Entertainment
   Arcades and Lounges
   Headliners and Major Attractions

Retail Shopping
Operations Support
Conclusion

INTRODUCTION

Larger casinos often offer meeting, event, convention, and entertainment facilities to attract new customers. These added services expand the range of attractions to entice gamblers to the facility, and to encourage customers to stay longer. The meeting space is used to bring in groups who will spend large blocks of time in the resort facility. Meetings and conventions occur during the week when casinos are slowest, so they are a good use of space. Plus, the conventioneers may be new to the facilities so if they enjoy themselves, they may become repeat guests. While the conventioneers' primary activity may not be gambling, it is anticipated that they will spend some time in the casino. Most people attending meetings also stay in the casino hotel and eat in the restaurants, paying full price. Therefore, meetings and conventions are good business for the resort operations, and attendees are potential gamblers in the casino.

The entertainment is designed to attract individuals, couples, and families from outside the casino (Figure 6.1). Many of the in-house guests (tourists) enjoy the entertainment as part of their stay. On the other hand, locals are also attracted by the entertainment venue and come to see the show. Many entertainment customers, who are outsiders to the casino, will gamble while waiting for the entertainment to begin and will linger in the casino afterward.

MEETING AND CONVENTION FACILITIES

Meeting Room Facilities

The range of meeting and convention facilities varies widely in casinos. Many casinos have smaller meeting rooms to accommodate business meetings and small social events (Figure 6.2). The rooms are usually decorated with wall-to-wall carpet, attractive

FIGURE 6.1   Showgirls in a casino entertainment production.

Source: Getty Images, Inc.

FIGURE 6.2   Rendition of a medium-sized meeting room set up theater style.

Source: Image from BigStockPhoto.com.

wallpaper and mirrors, and high ceilings. The rooms are generally equipped with several sets of lights to accommodate bright settings for meetings, and softer settings for dinners and socials.

Often these smaller meeting rooms have at least one modular wall that rolls back into the main wall so that two or more meeting rooms can be combined to create larger spaces. Frequently, a casino will have one large ballroom that can be subdivided into these smaller meeting spaces as needed. The ballroom can be used for major events. Mid-sized events can use half of the ballroom, allowing the casino to subdivide the other half into smaller spaces.

To anticipate the varying needs of groups using the meeting spaces, the casino maintains a stewarding staff. The **stewards** are responsible for setting up the meeting room according to a client's request. For example, chairs can be brought into the space to set the room up **theater style**, which means there are many rows of chairs facing the same end of the room in a style similar to a movie theater. At the front of the room, a lectern is provided so that speakers can address the group comfortably. Audio/video (A/V) equipment is provided as needed. This style is preferred for lectures, motivational speakers, presentations, and so on where the focus is upon one person at the front of the room and the participants don't need to take notes, work with materials, and so on.

Another common setting might be the **classroom style**, which entails setting up long tables in rows with two or three chairs at each table. All of the tables face the front of the room in the same style as a school classroom so that all participants face forward. A lectern and A/V equipment is provided at the front of the room for a trainer, speaker, or lecturer. This room setting is often preferred for training sessions or workshops where participants need the table space to work with materials.

A third common meeting room setup style is that of a **boardroom**. Tables are grouped together in the middle of the room and chairs are arranged around the outside perimeter of the tables. This arrangement enables all participants to face one another across the tables. Audio/video equipment can be provided as needed. This setting enables the group to have a more intimate environment for their meeting, allowing for easier face-to-face interactions. Conversation is easier, too, as the participants are closer together compared to the other setup styles.

In addition to the stewarding staff to set up the meeting rooms as desired by the clients, the casino needs a **convention sales staff** to handle the bookings of the meeting rooms. This sales staff answers customer inquiries, coordinates requests for services, confirms reservations, collects advance deposits, and so on. The sales staff also oversees the events, so the staff often works day and evening shifts, seven days a week. Therefore, the sales staff works two shifts per day so that customers can reach them. Further, the casino sales staff wants to be as available as possible so they accommodate the four major time zones of the United States. Typically, the sales office is open every day from 7 A.M. until 11 P.M. (occasionally later if the event requires it).

Convention Facilities

Conventions are very large events that typically involve many people and extend over several days. There are many types of conventions. The most common are trade shows and conferences. **Trade shows** are large gatherings where vendors bring their newest products and services to display, demonstrate and sell.

Booths are often set up in a large hall so that visitors can wander the aisles to view the different vendor offerings (Figure 6.3). The casino can earn money by selling the

FIGURE 6.3 Bally Street booth setup for Bally Equipment Corporation at a trade show.

booths to vendors, plus the various services each vendor may desire. For example, some vendors require tables to display equipment, brochures, and so on. These tables are outfitted with skirts to make them more attractive, and to provide storage space under the table for the vendor. Some vendors occasionally need electricity for their booths, so the casino can sell electrical wiring and power. Other vendors may want carpeting, special lighting, and so on, which the casino can also provide, charging only for the services that each vendor requests. In addition to selling services to individual vendors who purchase booth space, the casino also charges the sponsoring association for broad services such as use of the large room, utilities to cover heating or cooling, security staff, special signage, use of restrooms, and so on.

The other common type of convention is the **conference**. In this type of large meeting, speakers use a series of small meeting rooms to give lectures or otherwise share information (Figure 6.4). There are typically several sessions all day long, and attendees can move between sessions, finding ones of personal interest. The attendees may pay the sponsoring organization a registration fee for participating. In such cases, the sponsoring organization is the client of the casino. All services provided for the conference are billed to the sponsoring organization. Participants are not charged anything directly by the casino for the conference activities. The range of services is similar to that of a trade show, but booths are rarely used. Instead, small meeting rooms are set up, either in classroom or theater style, to facilitate the lectures and workshops.

Other large gatherings may be **special events**. These events are usually unique and generally open to the public. Special events can be repeated similar to trade shows and conferences, but the difference is the target population. Trade shows are generally focused upon one industry such as computer manufacturers or accountants or restaurant equipment. Conferences are generally held for members of an association, industry, or even one large firm. In both cases, the participants have something in common. In contrast, the

FIGURE 6.4 Gaming industry annual convention.

special event is usually open to the general public. It doesn't target one particular group but rather hopes to appeal to everyone. Either the casino or the sponsoring agency (client), depending upon how it is negotiated with the casino convention sales staff, may sell tickets for entry. Some events may have a limit on the number of participants. An example of this is a musical concert where seating is fixed and limited. Other types of special events include announcements of new products, sporting events such as boxing, or theatrical performances.

There are many different purposes for meetings, conventions, or special events. However, casinos are interested in hosting them because each event brings potential gamblers into the casino for several hours. Patrons are encouraged to gamble both before and after the event. The walkways to the event locations are often woven past banks of slot machines and are often in sight of the table games. While entrances to the events may be through limited doorways for ticketing reasons, there are usually many more exits so that patrons can exit the event venue quickly. Of course, these exits all channel patrons back through the gaming areas of the casino. The events draw the people to the casino. The games are made as available as possible for players' convenience.

There is a historical feeling about conventions held at casinos. Attendees know in advance the locale is a casino. This helps them prepare for the casino experience. The participants often plan to participate in the event but also often plan to gamble as well. The current reaction to casinos is generally positive so attendees often look forward to both the event that draws them to the casino and the gambling experience, too.

ENTERTAINMENT

Providing customers with entertainment helps to keep them in the casino for a longer period of time. It also often draws people who want to enjoy the entertainment as their primary reason for visiting. The range of entertainment spans a wide variety of choices. Entertainment can include game arcades, small lounge shows, large concerts with headliners (well-known celebrity performers), and even thrill rides and other automated attractions.

Arcades and Lounges

Game arcades are designed to attract young adults and families with teens. Popular video games, pinball machines, and interactive machines such as for dancing, auto racing, and so on are typical options. Some casinos provide automated games that appeal to younger children, too. The arcades provide minors with a place to entertain themselves while their parents are gambling. A casino employee is often assigned to make change, keep the area clean, help identify machines needing repair, and so on.

Because of the frequent presence of minors, the security employees pay close attention to the gaming arcade. Regular patrols of uniformed security staff are made so that a visible presence is maintained in addition to the casino employee supervising the area. The Surveillance department also keeps an eye on the arcade via cameras. This focus upon the arcade helps to provide appropriate supervision of the arcade area for the protection of the minors.

Young adults often patronize the arcades, too. While many are of legal age and can gamble, often this age group seeks other activities to stay entertained. The gambling is often fun, but young adults also look for other diversions for enjoyment. More complex

FIGURE 6.5   Typical lounge act as free entertainment for gamblers.

Source: Image from BigStockPhoto.com.

arcade games are installed to challenge these older players. Some games are competitive so that you can race a car against your friends in their cars via a simulation racetrack. It can also be used as family entertainment as grandpa, dad, and son can all compete against one another with cars, target practice, or adventure simulations. Although all games are offered for a small charge, none of the machines are used for gambling. The fees paid are strictly for the play of the arcade game with no financial reward for high performance.

Lounge shows are a regular form of entertainment within casinos. Offered both at nights and during some afternoons, the purpose of the lounge shows is to give gamblers something to do between gambling sessions. Players do get tired if sitting at a slot machine or table game for an extended period of time. The lounge shows give players a pleasant diversion while keeping them inside the casino.

Lounge shows can be any type of small, limited performance (Figure 6.5). They can be a solo performer, duo, or trio singing songs. They can be small bands playing music with or without a live vocal performer. Sometimes a casino will bring in a stand-up comedian to entertain the players. The concept is to create an intimate setting for up to 50–60 people in a bar setting. Patrons can order beverages or appetizers, play video poker at the bar, or sit at tables to just relax and enjoy.

Headliners and Major Attractions

To stimulate more interest and attract large numbers of visitors, casinos may feature a headliner. A **headliner** is a famous performer with wide name recognition who easily attracts audiences from distant places. Examples include Barbra Streisand, Diana Ross (formerly of the Supremes), Celine Dion, and Wayne Newton. Sometimes the headliner performs for a limited period of time such as a few weeks. Other times the headliner performs for years. The duration of the show depends upon the interest and availability of the performer and the casino's assessment of the drawing power of the performer over time.

Barbra Streisand and Diana Ross typically perform for very limited engagements. While the short duration doesn't bring many visitors to the casino over time, for those short periods the casino is sold out for the concerts and full with many gamblers in the casino, the restaurants, and hotels. The headliners are promoted aggressively, not only to sell out the concert itself, but also to promote the casino brand name.

Other headliners agree to perform for many years. An example is Wayne Newton. He moved to Las Vegas and performs at the MGM Grand. During the last 40 years he has performed over 30,000 solo acts in Las Vegas. He has built up a very loyal fan base. Many of the fans repeat their visits. Called "Wayne-iacks," they often compete to see how many times they can see his show. A number of fans have seen the show 500 or more times (Figure 6.6). Some have even seen his performance more than 2,000 times!

Celine Dion performed in Las Vegas from 2003 through 2007 at Caesar's Palace. Initially she had a three-year commitment, but she was such a success that her contract was extended for two more years. Her act was the sixth-highest selling show in both 2005 and 2006, and sold out almost every night during the five years. Her notoriety brought more name recognition to both herself as a performer and to Caesar's Palace as the place where she performed. In spite of some complaints about the higher ticket prices for her show, the extravaganza generated strong profits and a regular parade of visitors to Caesar's Palace.

Because of the high expense of famous headliners, many casinos have resorted to extravaganzas that do not have a famous person in the lead. Instead, choreographers use elaborate sets and large casts of unknown dancers and show girls to entertain. Many mechanical sets are added to amaze audiences. The very high cost of the headliner is eliminated. The added costs of the larger casts and the mechanical equipment are still less than the cost of a headliner. The combination of many performers dancing and singing, backed

FIGURE 6.6 Concert ad of upcoming entertainment at the Rainbow Casino in Wendover, Nevada.

FIGURE 6.7 Casino marquee promoting entertainment.

up by music and moving sets, has been very successful in attracting regular visitors and potential gamblers. Some casinos have created their own Broadway style shows as well (Figure 6.7).

Thrill rides and attractions are other forms of entertainment that some casinos add to attract potential gamblers. The New York New York Hotel and Casino in Las Vegas has a roller coaster that winds over and around the casino building. Up the strip from the New York New York is the Stratosphere Casino. It has a tall tower with a revolving restaurant at the top. Above the restaurant is a platform that is structured for three amusement rides. Customers can enjoy the "Big Shot," a catapult that launches passengers straight up 160 feet at 45 mph (a g-force over 4), which takes them 1,081 feet above the Las Vegas strip. Another option is the "X-Scream," which is a teeter-totter that propels passengers 27 feet over the edge of the tower, at an attitude of 866 feet above the ground. The third option is "Insanity, the Ride," which is a massive mechanical arm that extends 64 feet over the edge of the tower and spins passengers at a g-force of 3. Instead of having headliners to draw crowds, the Stratosphere uses these thrill rides to attract regular crowds to its facility (Figure 6.8).

The engineering of both attractions and performances has led to the development of a professional staff within the casino to build and maintain the sets, machines, and support equipment needed to regularly operate the shows and attractions. These technicians require specialized skills. In addition, directors and choreographers are needed to design and manage the various shows. These employees are essential to the regular operation of the shows and attractions that draw new and repeat customers to the casino facility.

FIGURE 6.8   Big Shot thrill ride at the top of the Stratosphere Hotel and Casino in Las Vegas.

Source: © Dorling Kindersley, Courtesy of Stratosphere, Las Vegas.

Some casinos pride themselves in sports venues like boxing matches. Others like in Pennsylvania have live horse racing with slot machines called "**racinos**." However, in addition many casinos offer the full range of recreational activities like golf, bowling alleys, swimming, and health clubs. One of the newest trends is the addition of spas to a resort. Many tourists enjoy going for a manicure, pedicure, massage, facial, or just spending the afternoon or day enjoying many different services. Both women and men enjoy spending time relaxing with these various services. In addition, spas bring in locals who come for the services and may spend more time at the resort or casino.

RETAIL SHOPPING

Shopping is also considered a form of entertainment for casino patrons. Building upon the concept of giving gamblers options to entertain themselves while taking a break from gambling, shopping arcades have been created to attract customers. Many shops are interesting and unusual boutiques that offer clothing, fine art, and other unusual items. Sundry shops provide basic needs such as shampoos, toothpaste, paperback books, newspapers, and souvenirs (Figure 6.9).

The boutiques often offer a wide range of shopping options, from upscale clothing and shoes to jewelry, furs, and fine art. Most of the items are priced at the upper end with the idea that big winners in the casino have someplace to spend their winnings. Frequently the boutiques are grouped together so that a small shopping arcade is formed, enabling customers to stroll about, looking at the fine products and watching other shoppers who are making purchases. Celebrating victories, presenting eye-catching store windows, and selling top-end products often add a sense of luxury, prestige, and glamour to the gaming experience. Retail shopping malls have also become a big attractor for the casinos drawing in tourists as well as locals. The Caesars Forum, the Grand Canal, and the

FIGURE 6.9   Marble floors and a glass ceiling house elegant stores at Via Bellagio, a shopping arcade in the Bellagio in Las Vegas.

Source: Alan Keohane © Dorling Kindersley.

Desert Passage are all major shopping draws for guests in Las Vegas. Remember, it doesn't really matter which venue guests spend their time and money, so long as they have a great time because all the money comes back to the casino resort operations.

OPERATIONS SUPPORT

To support the meetings, conventions, special events, and entertainment, the casino resort quite often creates several special departments to control and operate all these different venues. As a result, a large portion of the Marketing and Sales department of the resort provides support to handle marketing, finance, and accounting transactions. Typically, these are in addition to the casino marketing staff who promote casino special events like slot and poker tournaments that are created to draw gamblers to the casino. (For more information about these operations, *Casino Marketing: Theories and Applications*, discusses these activities in this series.) The purpose is to (1) generate new visitors to the resort and (2) promote the brand name. Adding the promotion of events and entertainment can make the marketing strategy much more complex. Frequently, additional marketing staff are added who concentrate exclusively upon events and entertainment. While not always the case, having this additional staff in the same department as the casino marketing staff enables a strong coordination between promotion of the casino and of the events and entertainment. It avoids having two Marketing departments (resort and casino) from conflicting with one another when making plans for special events.

FIGURE 6.10   The marketing staff works to coordinate financial and accounting records of a major event.

The financing of events and entertainment can require the casino to provide services and equipment well in advance of the actual dates of the event. The Finance department works with the operational staff and the marketing staff to coordinate the provision of funding of the events. The convention sales staff may arrange for deposits in advance of events, but the finance staff needs to know about this to incorporate the flow of cash. Advertising requires payment in advance. Arranging the flow of cash is an important aspect of financial management. The Accounting department is important in the tracking of sales and expenses. With so many different contracts negotiated by the convention sales staff with varying terms and conditions, the Accounting department records each transaction, aiding the accurate recording of each sales activity. Determining the profitability of each operation is essential for management (Figure 6.10).

Interdepartmental coordination becomes an important aspect of managing the casino resort when meetings, special events, concerts, shows, and shopping are all operating in the facility. Since the events are offered to draw customers, coordinating with all other departments within the resort is necessary. These events have an impact upon traffic flow in and around the resort. Security is involved to help control parking and public transportation access outside the resort as well as controlling crowds within. The food service outlets need to be prepared for more customers. Sufficient food has to be on hand to fill orders, and enough staff has to be scheduled to handle the volume of customers. The hotel needs to know well in advance so it can plan to accommodate bookings for the event. The Maintenance department needs to know so that it can be prepared to handle any emergency repair needs. With larger quantities of people in the building than usual, the air cooling or heating may need adjustment. Electrical power usage often increases during special events (lighting, special equipment for the shows, air handling systems, etc.), and quick repairs to blown circuits, overheated fixtures, and so on may be vital to the success of the event or for public safety. Even the casino cashier cage needs to be aware of the potential influx of customers so that sufficient money and gambling chips are on hand.

The starting and ending time of the event needs to be known so these departments can anticipate when the extra business will occur. Estimating when customers will begin to arrive before the event is important to traffic management, restaurant activity, and hotel registration. Knowing when the event is scheduled to end helps anticipate when and how the visitors will either leave the building or enter the casino to gamble, walk into the restaurants and bars to eat or drink, or to enjoy many of the other services in the resort complex.

Conclusion

The purpose of these extra services—meetings, conferences, conventions, all entertainment, and shopping—is to bring additional visitors into the casino. As discussed elsewhere in this book, casinos operate on volume. The earnings per game are fairly fixed. Having masses of players gamble is what creates the profit for the casino. Using conventions, entertainment, and shopping as tools to attract players is an important marketing tool as well as a potential profit maker for the casino.

Key Words

Stewards *59*
Theater style *59*
Classroom style *59*
Boardroom *59*

Convention sales staff *60*
Trade shows *60*
Conference *61*
Special Event *61*

Lounge show *63*
Headliner *63*
Racinos *66*

Review Questions

1. Write an overview of meeting and convention facilities and entertainment as part of the gaming industry.
2. Discuss the qualities and features of meeting room facilities.
3. Discuss the qualities and features of convention facilities.
4. Detail the qualities and features of arcades and lounges and their contributions to casino operations.
5. Detail the qualities and features of headliners and major attractions and their contributions to casino operations.
6. Describe how retail shopping contributes to casino operations.
7. Write an overview of operations support.

CHAPTER 7

CASINO CULTURE

KATHRYN HASHIMOTO

Learning Objectives

1. To provide an overview of recent trends in casino culture[1]
2. To learn the trend of the perception of casinos from criminal to respectable
3. To learn about the trend of casino operations from low tech to high tech
4. To learn the evolution of playing tools, mechanicals, and surveillance in casino operations
5. To learn the trend of casinos attracting individual gamblers to masses of gamblers
6. To learn about the trend of individual business owners to team management of casinos
7. To learn about the shift in casinos to team management and corporate culture
8. To understand the development of the clash between tradition and corporate culture in the casino industry

Chapter Outline

Introduction
The Trend from Criminal to Respectable
The Trend from Low Tech to High Tech
  Playing Tools
  Mechanicals
  Surveillance
The Trend from Targeting Individuals to Masses
The Shift from Individual Business Owners to Team Management
The Shift to Team Management and Corporate Culture
  Tradition versus Corporate
Conclusion

INTRODUCTION

In American history, the gambling spirit is said to be inherent in the culture. It took a special breed of individual to come from England and settle the American wilderness: a gambling person, someone willing to take a risk to improve one's lot in life. Because settlements were few and far between, many people settled on land far from their neighbors. Because the nearest person could be hundreds of miles away, tools and equipment were needed to lighten the workload. In order to develop the land for cultivation, new types of plows needed to be developed which could easily be fixed and transported through forests to get to their final destination. The new frontier required a gambling person who could create and improve on previous inventions to meet new challenges. Therefore, technology, culture, and the gambler developed together in the need to succeed and improve life in America. As the New World became more populated, people continued to take risks and invent new things to make their lives easier.

There have been four major trends that have spanned American culture and influenced the development of gaming and casinos: the trend from being an outlaw to being respectable; from being a low-tech culture to being a high-tech culture; from a focus on the individual to a focus on the masses; and from the rise of individual business owners to the rise of team management. Each of these trends started with sole backwoods pioneers with bare minimum technology, and developed into groups of hi-tech people wanting and using sophisticated tools to make a difference (Figure 7.1).

FIGURE 7.1 Showing the joy of success sought by gamblers.

Source: Image from BigStockPhoto.com.

THE TREND FROM CRIMINAL TO RESPECTABLE

Historically, gambling has been associated with shysters, conmen, and criminals. For example, in the case of the lottery, conmen have always managed to build a successful lottery system so that they could later abscond with any proceeds. Even in Colonial times, gambling was an important fact of everyday life. In order to outfit the voyage of the *Mayflower*, a lottery was conducted to raise the necessary money. Although the organizers were eventually run out of town on a rail for cheating, there was enough money raised to get the expedition started. Later, when infrastructure was needed to develop New England towns, a lottery was created to fund the needed projects. The scoundrels who ran them were eventually found out, and the lottery was disbanded. Later during the Civil War, the Louisiana Lottery was created to help Charity Hospital with expenses. As part of the contract, the managers could keep any money that was not needed by the hospital. Until current times, this was the largest lottery in the United States, infamously known as "**the octopus**," because its tentacles of corruption were so widespread. Eventually, sheriffs had to come from Washington to disband the operations for fraud.

Later, as Nevada became the playground for the California elite, **Bugsy Siegel** was purported to have created the idea of gambling in the desert. Unfortunately, he is also alleged to have gained his fortune by founding "Murder Inc." for the mob. He also used mob money to market and build the first casino there. It failed when the social elite deserted him on opening night because they did not want to be publicly associated with gangsters. While Bugsy met his demise by his own company, the idea of casinos and fun in the desert was a success. Since the mob had a great deal of money to spend and launder at the time, Las Vegas casinos were a great investment. As Nevada prospered, so did the gangsters. Thus, the criminal aspect of gambling has long been a part of American culture.

However, in the 1960s, as the story goes, **Howard Hughes** liked the penthouse suite at one of the casinos so much that he wanted to stay there all the time. Penthouse suites are for high rollers—people who spend large amounts of money gambling. The casino management wanted to throw Hughes out because he didn't spend enough in the casino. Finally, one day, a manager probably told him, "Look, this is company policy. You can't stay here and live. You have to leave." Now, company policies were things that Hughes could understand as a business tycoon. So, he probably told the manager, "Change the policy." The corresponding reply was something like "If you're so hot on changing the policy, you try." So, Hughes bought the casino and did change the policy. About this time, **William Harrah** began to develop his casino/hotels. It wasn't hard for other major corporate geniuses to realize that casinos were a gold mine. However, the reputation of gambling and casinos needed some work. Therefore, Harrah and the other corporations began to work with government to get rid of the gangsters. For example, in the late 1960s, Nevada law was changed to permit corporate ownership of casinos rather than only individual ownership. This was the beginning of respectability for the casino industry.

The corporate tycoons began to run the casinos like traditional big business operations. Big business meant automated systems. The new computerized systems improved efficiency and minimized possible discrepancies in transactions such as illegal manual entries. Auditing also became easier. The Nevada Gaming Commission required that casinos maintain a minimum of seven years of reports. As you can imagine, these records filled enormous underground vaults. Eventually, all that paper became small CDs with quick-backup data files and continuous upload and download capabilities. Now, satellites allow data to be stored elsewhere with multiple collecting sites so that there is no downtime for backups. This allows for an extra level of security in that multiple copies of the data can be stored at many different locations. If something were to happen to the data at one site, there would be another backup of the data at one of the other locations. Linked gaming systems now allow accounting and security management systems to be checked by governmental jurisdictions. Regulators can control illegal machine gambling by licensing, regulating, and monitoring machine play. The central computer systems continuously monitor the network to linked terminals, assuring that the wide varieties of games are fair and honest. In fact, the use of technology by governmental agencies to monitor such activities is quickly becoming a necessity due to the large number of activities that need to be monitored and the increased sophistication of illegal activities. These monitoring systems often include basic forms of artificial intelligence in order to help spot illegal activity that may not be easily recognized (Figure 7.2).

Seeing the money that casinos can generate, Atlantic City developers began to explore their options. Originally an elegant seaside resort for New York City residents to cool their summers, by the 1960s, increased tourist travel by planes and trains had eroded Atlantic City's clientele. As one reporter put it, "It is a slum by the sea." How could the city be revitalized? Gambling came to mind, but there was a deep concern about mob control of the casinos. Whereas Nevada regulations had been laissez faire, New Jersey gaming regulations were written as ultraconservative. They created an abundance of laws and regulations to make casinos toe the line for respectability. Then, as Native American casinos and riverboats opened, people began to see that casinos were respectable. As Steve Wynn said "Casinos are recreation and entertainment." The high point of respectability was Steve Wynn's award for "1994 Independent Hotelier of the World." Casinos are now so accepted and respectable that casino stocks are traded on Wall Street.

FIGURE 7.2 Shuttle busses transport patrons to parking lots at large casinos.

THE TREND FROM LOW TECH TO HIGH TECH

Playing Tools

Traditionally, gambling consisted of the easiest accessible materials: dice and cards. For example, craps was a very popular street game. All a player needed was a pair of dice and money (Figure 7.3). Dice fit comfortably inside a gentleman's pants pocket. A deck of cards is also easily obtainable and stored. In the Old West, a table and set of chairs were all that were needed to get a game started. Gambling and the Old West were almost synonymous: Think of the fabled card shark sitting at a table inside the saloon with his back to the wall, waiting for his prey to appear. There hasn't been a movie of the Old West made that didn't show some form of gambling as entertainment. As a result, many Americans have grown up playing poker of one type or another. The classic Broadway musical of the 1940s and 1950s, *Guys and Dolls,* was based around a craps player as the lead character. In the 1950s and 1960s, a weeknight out with the guys often meant playing poker. Low-tech games such as these were easily transportable, and one had only to reach into his/her pocket and a game was ready. After all, when a person was traveling by horse, and his belongings had to fit on a saddle, the practical aspect of gambling was important.

However, as America grew and became more civilized, the games became more sophisticated. The laws of probability were created by **Pascal** and used to learn how to win at cards. The playing style became more based on scientific thought, and the rules of the games adhered to those same laws. A good player knew the odds and bet accordingly. The

FIGURE 7.3 Lady luck is an important image at casinos.

Source: Image from BigStockPhoto.com.

table surfaces became fancier, with specialized layouts including betting circles. Also, the game rules and winnings became more easily available, directly in front of the player. Table games have become high tech. The simple house casino chip now has a radio frequency identification device (**RFID**) with a unique detail number for tracking. The tables now have slots for player cards, making it easier for the table games personnel to track information. However, with the sophistication of the Web, even casinos have become virtual reality programs. Internet gaming is the newest high-tech option in gambling development.

Mechanicals

In 1875, the Industrial Revolution manifested itself in the gambling industry with new gambling machines in which a person pulled a handle to set reels spinning. It was suggested that these **mechanical** devices would be good to occupy the women while the men gambled at the tables. By the 1930s, Jennings had developed the first electrically operated jackpot bell machine; now buttons could be pushed and gambling became much easier. In the 1970s, video poker was introduced. This machine was very popular because it gave players decision-making options and more buttons to push. People believed that the more buttons they controlled, the more their skill dominated their luck. Slot machines were becoming very popular.

In the 1980s, the evolution of the stepper slot allowed greater versatility and fewer parts to break down. Microprocessors enabled people to receive "credits" for their wins, resulting in less handling of the actual money and speeding up play. Although it had been thought that slots were more attractive for women because they were simple to learn, mechanicals (more affectionately called "one-armed bandits") rapidly grew to be the overall favorite over table games. By 1983, Nevada slot revenues surpassed table revenues. Many casinos found that slot revenues now comprised 60%–80% of the revenues, and the shift to add more slots and fewer table games ensued. The growth of the progressive IGT slot system in 1986 meant that people could win very large jackpots because the slot machines were linked to a central computer, and all bets were pooled into one large collective prize. Gaming machines were so popular that in early 1990, newer, larger denomination machines such as the $5, $25, $100, and even the $500 machine entered the market.

Gaming machines are now faster and allow for less failure in operations. The coin-acceptance devices have electric sensors to detect fake coins. A computer chip generates a series of random numbers and selects reel spin/stop sequences. In addition a liquid crystal display (LCD) computer chip allows diagnostic troubleshooting, bonus modes, and site-specific player information. A vacuum florescent display (VFD) displays the game information and diagnostic errors, and sets up informational messages. A player switch illuminates when coins are inserted or credits are won. Another chip records security violations and detects failures or errors. All the critical game data is stored in the random access memory (RAM) with a long-life battery attached so that data is not lost in case of a power failure.

Some of the newest technology in slot machines prints tickets containing all of a player's credits; the player does not have to carry around loose, heavy coins that can be dropped and lost. This also makes it easier for the casinos because they do not have to store vast numbers of rolls of quarters. This is especially helpful on riverboat casinos that are concerned about balancing the weight of the coins on their boats.

Finally, the slot machine data system enables all the information about every slot machine, every minute of the day, to be gathered and be available for analysis. Individual machines can be checked for cash flow, malfunctions, and security compromises. This technology was attempted in the mid-to-late 1960s but none of it was successful. Finally in 1973, Electro Module Inc., IBM, and Harvey's Wagon Wheel at Lake Tahoe developed the first viable system.

In 1974, Bally's acquired the rights to the **slot data system**. There are several components to the slot data system. The communicator is attached to the individual slot machine so that it can keep track of the coin flow. In addition, it monitors the machine for tampering, malfunctions, or other problems. Then, there is a card reader to identify employees and players. There is a program that displays the slot machine status data to the employees and also instructional and promotional material to the players. There is a computer interface unit that maintains communications between the central computer system and the slot machine. The interface unit also protects the system from transient voltages and electronic interferences. As a result, the slot data system functions in six basic areas: security, operations, maintenance, accounting, marketing, and management. With this hardware system in place, consultants or managers can apply new software to evaluate slot placement. These design programs can evaluate patrons, competitive situation marketing plans, and facility and types of games. Then a programmer can design products with each game type, cabinet style, and exact location on a screen with a scaled three-dimensional floor plan (Figure 7.4).

With the advent of computers, casinos have radically changed. Instead of a couple of tables on which to roll dice or play cards, heavy machinery has replaced many tables. Mechanicals have taken over the floor. Computer programs, digitized screens, and cashless payouts dominate the scene. Instead of the quiet bar with a hush in the room at a large bet, bells and whistles bounce off the walls and generate excitement. Computerized gambling machines with their sophisticated microprocessors also allowed new and creative games to be developed. Today any table game can be played on a video machine, which

FIGURE 7.4 An active blackjack pit showing dealers at work at the Bellagio in Las Vegas, Nevada.

Source: Peter DaSilva/The New York Times/Redux.

reduces the number of personnel needed to operate a casino. However, the downside is that these machines require trained, experienced computer programmers, who are expensive to hire, to repair any problems.

Surveillance

America's early history is depicted in movies of the Old West with John Wayne as cowboy. The scene is tense as the bad guys with the black hats wait in the saloon with a marked deck of cards for some sucker to enter. Up above on the second-floor balcony sits a man with a shotgun. He protects the owner below. As people enter, the protector stands up and walks slowly back and forth along the railing, keeping an eye on troublemakers. This was the beginning of surveillance from above.

In later developments, as casinos became more sophisticated, the balcony walkway became an intricate grid above the entire floor of the casino. These catwalks allowed surveillance to be hidden from view, but everything on the casino floor to be seen. Unfortunately, the viewing required darkness in the catwalk area, so a misstep could send a man crashing through the glass ceiling to the floor below. Catwalks had been in continuous use until the '90s when hi-tech equipment no longer required this secondary backup.

Another development in casino technology has been the rise of video cameras, which changed the way surveillance was conducted. These hi-tech cameras can focus so well that a surveillance person can see the date on a quarter at a table below. These cameras are strategically placed throughout the ceiling areas so that every square inch of casino floor space is covered by at least one camera at any given moment. To prevent a visitor from seeing where the cameras are pointing, the cameras are hidden by half-circles of smoked glass. Some of the newest technology has hidden cameras in statues and other places closer to the action. These cameras are connected to recording equipment that stores the floor information as long as necessary to catch cheaters or to prove cases in court. This information is stored digitally, which provides higher quality and greater durability than standard videotape. It also means those large vaults, cabinets, and closets for VCR tape storage were eliminated. As previously noted, the video data can now be uploaded to other sites for long-term storage.

For a long time, surveillance personnel carefully kept records of cheats in the "black books." However, computer links have changed all that. Now facial recognition programs can zoom in on a person, identify him/her, and determine whether surveillance should be concerned. Information on cheats and troublemakers is available globally so that tracking a roulette scam team or a notorious card cheat is easier. This allows surveillance to be aware of cheating teams who might be in the area, and to pass on this information to other casinos. This is an example of how competitors can also cooperate when it is in their shared best interest.

If casino personnel are puzzled about a situation or person, they can contact an independent surveillance team. These teams can link their computers with the casino cameras to see all the action without even being in the same town. The video feed can also be passed on to experts anywhere in the world. If a casino suspects illegal activities, but are unsure, it is able to share that video feed with an expert on such activities by allowing him/her to view that video feed in real time via a virtual private network established over an Internet connection. Casinos no longer need to have someone with this level of expertise on the property at all times. An expert can be shared with several different casinos,

FIGURE 7.5   A woman holds a royal flush in hearts while gambling at a casino.

Source: Luc Beziat/Getty Images Inc.—Stone Allstoc.

which creates significant cost savings. This allows more eyes and more knowledge to be pooled toward protecting the casino and its customers (Figure 7.5).

Within the casino, software systems can also integrate with the security environment. They can show total dollars transacted through the games, monitor audits, and display employee transactions. These systems streamline operations by capturing image data, color portraits, and signatures to create identification cards and badges. They also use scans of employees' hands for payroll, for clocking in and out, and for restricting access to certain portions of the casino. This also has some application to the guest such as access to a hotel room or as identification in a casino for special privileges.

Another topic that is relatively new is radio frequency identification (RFID) tags. These tags are used in employee uniforms and on valuable pieces of equipment. This allows items to be tracked. Therefore, RFID tags can be somewhat controversial when they are used to track people, because of issues regarding invasion of privacy. The tags also allow employees to swipe cards at cash registers in the cafeteria, making it easier and quicker to get meals. In addition, the software can facilitate the monitoring of staff levels as well as discriminate between active and former employees. All the specific information about each employee is entered into computers and stored for instantaneous retrieval when necessary.

As a result of all these changes from low technology to high technology, the casino culture had to alter as well. New departments were added to address the repair issues, and people had to become knowledgeable about computers. In order to run these computer-driven programs, managers needed more technical backgrounds and a better understanding of the big picture that the computers could bring to the table. Data is now available instantly to assess problems. Information of all kinds is accessible with a push of a button. As a result, unlike in the past where a manager needed to have a pair of dice, a deck of cards, and a loyal shotgun security person on the balcony, a manager today must be able to juggle knowledge about computer programs, vast information availability, and the big picture of how everything fits together.

THE TREND FROM TARGETING INDIVIDUALS TO MASSES

Throughout American history, men gambled to pass the time and to make a few dollars. In the past, only men were considered to be gamblers. However, they came with women who had to be entertained. Women sometimes disturbed gamblers' concentration by asking for money to do other things such as go shopping, find something to eat, or be entertained. Women had to do this because it was believed that "nice girls" did not gamble. Originally it was thought that mechanical devices called "slots" would be the perfect entertainment for these women. While they were using them, they could have free food and drink and they could spend money. These women were probably the first "low rollers." However, casinos began to realize that low rollers could also contribute to a casino's profitability. As corporations such as McDonald's have learned, having more clients spending fewer dollars equals a few clients spending many dollars. This philosophy meant that rather than all the casinos going after the same 100 "whales" (people with millions to bet), the market opened up to all people over 21 years of age. The first method to draw low rollers was created by casinos in Atlantic City when they developed chartered bus programs. Bus companies charge a small amount of money, say, for example, $30. The $30 would include the bus ride, drinks, food, and entertainment during the ride; free buffet coupons at the casino; and $20 in slot tokens.

The casinos knew how to attract high rollers and low rollers, but what about the bulk of Middle America? How could casinos identify these people and then track them for "comps" (complimentary or free stuff) in order to get them onto the floor? Computers made this an easy market to attract. First is the problem of identifying Middle America: Tell people the casino wants to give them "comps," but the casino needs to know how to reach them to send them the coupons and free offerings. Thus, player's clubs were created as a marketing tool. Newcomers stop by the player's club booth and sign up by giving the casino their personal and financial information. In exchange, the players put their player's club card in the slot machine to measure their rate of play. Simple. The people voluntarily give the casino important personal information that allows it to develop a database of clients, and then people use the club card, which shows the casino exactly how much the player is worth. The player's club card inputs time spent at each machine, how much money was bet, and the overall amount of money spent per visit. This information is necessary for the player rating systems. Now everyone over 21 can be evaluated and tracked for his/her value to the casino. The information gathered from the players along with other information gathered from other electronic databases allows a casino to develop an effective marketing campaign to attract players, especially those considered to be of high value to the casino. Casinos have also integrated this information with their customer relationship management (**CRM**) systems to become even more sophisticated in providing excellent service to their guests, which in turn helps create life-long customers.

Now that the system within the casino is in place, how do you attract and inform the masses that the casino has all these wonderful opportunities available to them? One way is Web sites. The goal of a Web site should be to educate and help visitors with their questions. This is important because the number one reason people visit Web sites is to get information. Within the Web site, information should encourage visitors to return frequently to the Web site for new information, while obtaining their personal data and permission to contact them. The more visits the same person makes to the Web site, the more opportunities the casino has to learn about their wants and desires in food and beverage, their social habits, or their physical or spectator activities—in other words, their demographic and psychographic profiles. These facts allow a casino to create offers that are interesting to specific customers. Web visitors are open to information because they actively instigated the contact to know more about the casino. This is an excellent opportunity for the casino to obtain permission from Web visitors to increase their level of contact by offering to send a newsletter or e-mailing them special offers and marketing materials. This request allows visitors to "buy into" the process. On the flip side, every communication must always offer the option to "unsubscribe," so the goodwill that is created will not be tarnished by the visitors' frustration at receiving materials without any choice. Keep in mind that the objective is to help the visitor with his/her desire for more information, not to deliver a sales pitch. This form of Web site marketing allows casinos to create a database that grows richer in information every day. As more information is known about a specific person, the marketer can divide people into special segments based upon their needs and can tailor offers to match their desires.

Another benefit of these databases is their use in building brand-loyalty programs. The objective of these programs is to offer clients a package that will perfectly fit their needs. Because they feel that the casino knows and cares about their wishes, customers become brand loyal. However, one of the biggest concerns of player's club members is that they get offers that are not relevant to them. For example, a member wagered in excess of $10,000 when in Detroit on business; however, the member lived in California. A month later, he received a dinner coupon good for two people. This offer is not going to entice someone from California to venture back to Detroit. He needs at least a room and a meal. Another example: a regular tournament player frequents the local casino and spends $5,000 on an average visit, betting $25 a hand. All the dealers and pit bosses know him on sight. Yet, rather than ask him what he would like as a package, he receives offers for dinner for two. These offers are very standard and very unimaginative. Both men feel that the casino does not care about their business because they didn't bother to find out what they each really wanted and needed. As a result, they are not brand-loyal customers, but they could have been given time to explore their needs. Technology is a wonderful tool if used correctly. However, when dealing with people, it still comes back to getting to know the customer and personalizing the offers.

With the major shift from a few gamblers to the thousands of people who walk through casino doors each day, the casino rapidly altered from small simple buildings to massive complex buildings with spas, retail malls, multiple F&B outlets, and some of the largest hotels in the world. In the beginning, managers/owners simply waited in the bar for the gamblers to arrive. Now there are computers and marketers who look at geographic segments and psychological preferences to decide what people the managers and owners want to draw to the casino. Because of the sophistication and complexity of the operations to attract players, the casino culture also changed to a "people-driven" focus. Included in this mix is the emphasis on employees as motivated people who create the welcoming culture for the guests.

THE SHIFT FROM INDIVIDUAL BUSINESS OWNERS TO TEAM MANAGEMENT

In America, the history and evolution of casinos have created two very strong organizational cultures: individual ownership and corporate ownership. An organizational culture could be described as the personality of the firm. Like a person, a business can be weak or strong, conservative or daring, even stodgy or innovative. Organizational cultures are very important because they set the boundaries for behavior by managers and employees. The stronger the culture, the easier it is for employees to know what they should do when the formal rules are not available. In casinos, there are always new situations and problems that must be addressed. A strong organizational culture sets the tone and guidelines for the problem solving and implementing solutions.

When casinos first developed in America, ownership was by a single individual who could lose that enterprise on a toss of the dice. It was the owner's "luck of the draw" that determined his length of stay, not his management ability. As a result, owners were superstitious and they trusted only their own instincts. The "**monopoly on brains**" syndrome referred to the fact that only the owner could make a great decision, not employees. Therefore the organizational culture was one of "Do as I say; I don't want to know your opinion." Management rested on one man's whim, not his management expertise or great management decision-making style (like most of business in those days, women were rarely in management or ownership positions). "Dummy up and deal" was the employee's slogan. Fear of management was what kept the employees honest. The individual owners and their traditional cultural practices believed that employees should be constantly reminded that their jobs were a privilege, not a right. Jobs could be taken away at any time. Promotion came to employees who were loyal to management. Employees had to learn the trade from the ground up, starting as a dealer and proving their knowledge and loyalty along the way.

In traditional cultural practices, superstition was as good a factor in making decisions as anything else. Therefore, women had a very small role to play. They were only decorations. Furthermore, they were thought to bring bad luck, so they were not good employees or gamblers. If they did appear, sexual harassment was to be expected. After all, what else was a woman good for in a casino? And if she didn't want that kind of attention, she wouldn't have walked in the door. African Americans were another group who faced superstitious discrimination. Until the late 1960s in Nevada, African-American employees and entertainers were not allowed to enter the front doors or drink out of cups reserved for the players; it was bad luck. However, the Rat Pack, that famous group of celebrity hipsters led by Frank Sinatra, changed this almost solely with their charisma. Their impressive ability to draw in money whether they were playing or working gave them the clout to alter policies driven by superstition and prejudice. They boycotted any casino where Sammy Davis, Jr., a very popular African-American entertainer and one of the Rat Pack, was not allowed. Their financial power and influence quickly changed policies.

During this time, employees showed their loyalty by doing whatever they could to help the owner. In some cases, employees were asked to violate rules and regulations in order to favor the house or accommodate a high-roller's desires. Even though guests might make unreasonable requests, operators would agree because the customer might take his business elsewhere. For example, at Caesars in Atlantic City, a customer requested that he have a male dealer instead of the woman who was currently at the table. The management complied, even though they knew that it was discriminatory. However, it was cheaper to pay the class action suit that followed than to antagonize the player.

Another way to show loyalty was to express extreme concern about the outcome of a game because it would be disloyal to want the customer to win. In addition, the dealer was perceived to be personally responsible for the outcome. After all, it was thought that some people were just "unlucky" and shouldn't deal certain games. Any dealer who lost money

FIGURE 7.6   Placing a large bet at the poker table.

Source: Image from BigStockPhoto.com.

had "bad karma" and was instantly fired: no questions asked. However, there were several ways to change bad luck. For example, changing the dice and/or cards would help change the luck of the casino. Changing out an "unlucky" (losing dealer) employee for a different one could also help improve a bad streak. One casino manager was reported to say, "It was a question of mind over matter." So, he would switch dealers with "weak minds" from a losing game. Without any rational decision-making guidelines, superstition and one man's version of common sense ruled the operations (Figure 7.6).

THE SHIFT TO TEAM MANAGEMENT AND CORPORATE CULTURE

During the 1960s and 1970s, there was a shift in management styles and decision making. Some say it was Howard Hughes who began the movement. Under his new management style, the casino functioned like any other large corporation. Superstitions were replaced by well-researched facts. Teams of employees replaced the individual owner. The idea that a dealer is responsible for the losses was replaced by probability theory. As a result, the casino made money and this encouraged other corporate giants like Baron Hilton to invest in casinos.

These giants of corporate America started a new trend in casino management styles and organizational cultures. The casino was divided into two parts: the casino side and the administration side. The casino side revolved around what happened on the casino floor: the daily grind of securing the casino and tracking the money. The management side handled the marketing, accounting, human resources, and so on. With this split, new emphasis was placed on educational backgrounds like MBAs. People with no background in gambling began to work on the marketing plans and run the financial enterprise. Computers and statistics became the guiding decision makers. For example, the responsibility for "comping" decisions switched from floor people to computers. When the old school lost their comping privileges to a computer, it was a confusing time. How could a computer know the right people to comp? How could a machine build a rapport with the players so that they would come back? Old-school supervisors issued comps to whomever they pleased; it gave them power. But now, the computer decided.

Tradition versus Corporate

The clash of traditional culture versus the new corporate culture was inevitable. The following sentiments characterize the traditional casino culture: "The guys upstairs don't know the business." "How can an MBA know anything about the way a casino works?" "If he/she doesn't understand the product, how can he/she manage it?" "They are just a bunch of kids with degrees but no real experience." "The only real way to learn the business is to start as a dealer and work your way up through the ranks." By the same token, members of the new corporate culture examined the traditional views and found them lacking. They would say things like: "The traditional managers want to micro-manage and keep everything to themselves." "They do not want anyone else to know what is going on." "This way of managing is out of date; they obviously haven't kept up with the times." "It's not necessary to be a dealer to run a company. What does a dealer know about marketing or accounting?" "Formal education is important. It teaches how to manage and oversee operations. It allows a person to step back and see the big picture." These statements reflected the new corporate culture.

Changing times reinforced the new casino corporate culture. However, it wasn't just the ownership switch that altered the traditional corporate culture. When Las Vegas and Atlantic City found themselves inundated with all kinds of new gaming venues, the competition for employees became intense. Finding trained employees was a big problem. Anyone with any qualifications or experience quickly climbed the corporate ladder, and there was always an enticement from the next casino or riverboat for higher wages. There were too many jobs and not enough workers. As a result, computer management tools became important. For example, gaming management systems united the departments. One system could be used for slot management, patron management, table games systems, cage and credit systems, and to integrate all that information into one database.

Conclusion

As American culture evolved, technology and gamblers have been an integral part of the development. The American spirit that was willing to take a chance developed into the American creative enterprise that invented newer and better tools to help people cope with their lives. After all, Americans say, "Necessity is the mother of invention," and that is true in the case of casinos. An exploration into the intertwining of culture, technology, and gambling suggests that there have been four major trends that have evolved throughout American history. Each one of them has created a unique style of management in casinos, and resulted in a highly technical environment where customers come to relax and be entertained.

Key Words

The octopus *72*

Bugsy Siegel *72*

Howard Hughes *72*

William Harrah *72*

Pascal *74*

RFID *75*

Mechanicals *75*

Slot data system *76*

CRM systems *79*

"Monopoly on brains" syndrome *81*

Review Questions

1. Write an overview of recent trends in casino culture.
2. Discuss the trend of the perception of casinos from criminal to respectable.
3. Discuss the trend of casino operations from low tech to high tech.
4. Discuss the evolution of playing tools, mechanicals, and surveillance in casino operations.
5. Discuss the trend of casinos attracting individual gamblers to masses of gamblers.
6. Discuss the trend of individual business owners to team management of casinos.
7. Describe the shift in casinos to team management and corporate culture.
8. Describe the development of the clash between tradition and corporate culture in the casino industry.

Endnote

1. The majority of this chapter first appeared in Hashimoto, K. (2008) Development of Corporate Culture and Technology. In *Casino Management: A Strategic Approach.* Prentice Hall: Columbus, OH. 247–270.

CHAPTER 8

LIFESTYLE IMPACT

CHRIS ROBERTS

Learning Objectives

1. To provide an overview of the casino's impact on lifestyles
2. To learn the impact of casinos on the lifestyles of customers
3. To understand the unique impact of casinos on the lifestyle of the out-of-town gambler
4. To understand the unique impact of casinos on the lifestyle of the local gambler
5. To learn of the impact of casinos on the lifestyles of casino employees
6. To understand the unique impact of casinos on the lifestyles of dealers
7. To understand the unique impact of casinos on the lifestyles of other casino employees

Chapter Outline

INTRODUCTION

Working or playing in a casino is a different experience than most others available to any of us in life. It's a world of fun, excitement, risk, and reward. When people enter a casino as customers, they seek a memorable experience. Some come to take great risks in order to potentially win a lot of money. Others come to just have fun while risking small sums of money, and with no real expectation of winning much, if anything. Some just come to be a part of the excitement. The reason for all people really boils down to one: it's an exciting experience that's different from daily life.

For the employees in the casino industry, the same is essentially true. These employees want to be "where the action is" and to share in the excitement, too. A key difference between service and manufacturing industries is that with service, such as casino resorts, production and consumption happen at the same time. The employees are right there with the customers. With manufacturing, a product is produced, boxed, and warehoused until purchased by a consumer. The consumer then takes the product to home or business where it is later consumed. The worker in the production process is nowhere near the product when it is used. In the service industry, the worker is right there with the customer, sharing in the ordering, delivery, and consumption processes.

At casino resorts, it is as fascinating to help provide the experience as it is to live it. Sure, there are daily routines that aren't very exciting, but it's those routines that help create and deliver the casino resort lifestyle. Being a worker in the resort means the employees share in the experience, too. They see the customers. They talk to the customers. They often interact with the customers over the course of many hours. A customer may even stay in the resort hotel, which means actually living there for a period of time. The enjoyment of the customers and their health and safety are immediate concerns requiring attention by all of the employees. The job, then, becomes a lifestyle because it is about creating a living experience for the customer, one that happens now, later today, and even tomorrow.

LIFESTYLES OF CUSTOMERS

As described earlier, the casino resort offers customers an experience across several dimensions of life. Customers can sleep overnight in the hotel, actually living at the resort. They can eat meals in the restaurants. They can attend shows, relax in the lounges with drinks, swim at the pool, or casually wander the retail shopping venues. Of course, customers can spend time at virtually any hour of the day or night in the casino, engaging in the excitement by placing bets at slots or table games, or sharing the excitement with friends by helping them to gamble, too. The casino resort experience is one that is available to customers for as little time or as much time as the customer wishes.

The average length of stay at Las Vegas casino resorts is three and a half days. During the 1990s, this market had positioned itself as a family destination on par with Walt Disney World in Florida or any similar family-oriented location. Families were encouraged to bring everyone—children, grandparents, and others. There were activities for all ages, including day-care facilities for the very young, video game arcades for teens, and of course 24-hour casinos for adults. The entertainment offered risqué shows for adults and more "G" rated shows for families such as Cirque du Soleil or Siegfried and Roy's magical spectacular with live tigers and other wild cats (Figure 8.1).

FIGURE 8.1 A winning blackjack hand at the Circus Circus Hotel and Casino in Las Vegas, Nevada.

Source: Alan Keohane © Dorling Kindersley.

In the new century, Las Vegas has changed this orientation to another theme: "What happens in Vegas, stays in Vegas." This message tells customers that they have refocused the market as an adult destination, where partying, celebrating, and gambling were to be unfettered experiences, and anyone's behavior would remain secrets that stayed in Vegas. While many of the activities for children disappeared, the large luxury resorts still remained and families continued to be welcomed. The concept of a family lifestyle event has shifted to one of primarily an adult locale, with adult activities, and where privacy would be protected.

What Las Vegas does usually spreads across the entire American gaming community. Casinos have successfully repositioned the gaming experience back to one for adults with betting, drinking, partying, and sex appeal. The lifestyle message is now about glamour; sex; fine dining; flashy entertainment; and money, money, and more money. It is supposed to be fun, wild, and crazy.

The Out-of-Town Gambler

The lifestyle for the out-of-town visitor to a casino resort is one of difference. The location is different: It's a place far from home. The accommodations are different: sleeping in a hotel instead of home. The restaurants and food are different: many unique eateries instead of eating at home. The clothing worn is different: The daily business outfit is set aside. On top of this, the community is oriented toward providing for this customer. Strangers aren't questioned, shunned, or cautiously viewed, but rather are expected, welcomed widely and warmly. Airports frequently have a number of visitor information booths and displays, advertisements for casino shows and other local activities, and even in some places such as Reno and Las Vegas, slot machines in the airport terminals!

Often, from the outside the casino resort building has a look of excitement and difference. The area around the casino resort community has a different feel. Out-of-town visitors often see buildings and images they don't see back home. American gaming communities such as Las Vegas, Reno, Atlantic City and Tupelo, Mississippi have structures that are distinctive and larger-than-life in many respects. Some of the casino resort buildings are very large because of the many hotel rooms attached to the building. The casino itself is often a larger building of several stories, resulting in an exterior surface that can be decorated with vivid colors, dramatic images, and symbols and letters that make it stand out from its surroundings. Several distinctive examples of this can be seen in Las Vegas. One is the **Luxor**, which is in the shape of a large pyramid, has an exterior surface entirely made of black glass, and has an extremely bright spotlight that shines from the top of the pyramid directly upward into the night. Another is **Excalibur**, which is built in the shape of a castle, complete with corner turrets and drawbridges, a large stone-block exterior facing, and pennants flapping from flagpoles at intervals around the top level. A third example is the New York New York casino resort. The entire building is sculpted as the New York City skyline (multiple skyscrapers of differing heights standing shoulder to shoulder) and it has a high-speed roller coaster wending its way over, above and around the buildings! These are certainly sites not found in typical American cities and towns (Figure 8.2).

The signage is usually very large, bright, flashy, and eye-catching. Often, the lettering is extremely large so that the words can easily be seen from a distance. Motorists who are rushing by in a speeding car can also see the signs and quickly read the message. Like the buildings, the signage is designed to inform quickly and to announce special events, showcase entertainment acts, and promote resort features and activities. Again, this approach to signage and advertising is generally different than in most American cities and towns. The-out-of town visitor is quickly given a sense that this experience will be distinctive.

These unusually designed buildings, bright countenances, and bold signage create a sense of an unreal reality for visitors. They know they are entering a world designed for fun and entertainment. Visitors know, and usually expect, that they will have unique

FIGURE 8.2 A croupier in the gaming room in the Casino de Hull just outside of Ottawa, Quebec, Canada.

Source: Alan Keohane © Dorling Kindersley.

FIGURE 8.3   Roulette and blackjack tables awaiting the arrival of customers.

Source: Image from BigStockPhoto.com.

experiences. They know what they do and see will be different from daily routines back home, and that memories will certainly be created (Figure 8.3).

The out-of-town visitor often shifts into a set of lifestyle behaviors that matches the sense of expectations created by the casinos. People begin to take more risks than they normally would. They gamble. They attend shows and other entertainment extravaganzas. They stay up late into the night, and frequently sleep later the next morning. They frequently eat more food than usual, drink more alcohol, and often sample menu selections well outside of their normal diets.

Personal image becomes much more important for many visitors. With so much money being gambled, or spent on fine dining and hotels, many out-of-town visitors want to convey a sense of success and wealth. They want to be viewed as someone who can easily afford to place big bets effortlessly and without concern. They want others—both other gamblers and casino workers—to view themselves as special, important and attractive; people to want to be around and to notice. They want to impress others.

Many casino resort guests wear clothes that are more relaxed in style, yet nice, during the day and often dress much nicer or more formally in the evenings. Women often wear more flashy outfits and add expensive and eye-catching jewelry. Men dress in upscale, better quality clothing to convey a sense of sophistication, elegance, and wealth—or at least convey a sense of success and comfort with spending money. It becomes an atmosphere where image is everything; of being recognized as well off economically; of having a station in life that means you belong in the casino resort environment; of being a Very Important Person (**VIP**).

The Local Gambler

In contrast to the out-of-town gambler, the local gambler isn't impacted much by the flash, glitz, and glamour. Many locals develop favorite places to gamble and eat that are quieter and less of a "tourist trap." Some casinos position themselves to cater to this market. The buildings tend to be smaller and more intimate. Customers get to know the employees better and build long-lasting relationships. Seeing a friendly, familiar face at one's favorite casino becomes an important part of the return visit for the local gambler, and this includes both casino employees and other local gamblers from the community. The experience is more of a social one rather than a life-altering, major vacation as it might be for the out-of-town gambler.

These local gamblers are more modest in their gambling yet tend to be more consistent as repeat customers over time. They build visiting a casino, gambling, and partaking of the dining and entertainment into a regular part of their normal lifestyle. Casino visits are not viewed as unusual, once-in-a-lifetime major event but rather as just another option for an afternoon or evening activity. Visiting a local casino becomes just one choice on par with going to see a movie, eating dinner at a local restaurant, attending a sporting event, or shopping at the local mall. For the local gambler, casinos are part of daily life, and visiting one is a fairly routine experience.

LIFESTYLES OF CASINO EMPLOYEES

Working in a casino resort is almost an unworldly experience. While many of the functions performed by employees are easily recognized and fairly mundane (waiting on tables, preparing food, cleaning hotel rooms, operating cash registers, etc.), a number of the other jobs are unique. Dealing blackjack for hours on end or managing a roulette table is certainly a task that one doesn't prepare for in most school systems and is not usually on lists of desired career roles. What makes the experience almost unworldly is the overall and constant effort to create a different experience for the gambling customer. It's about continually serving the customer. Employees are inculcated into the casino resort culture, which has a focus upon catering to the gambler so that he/she continues to gamble, has fun, and enjoys the experience. All functions, whether directly related to gambling, or connected to other services such as food and beverage, lodging, entertainment, or shopping, are designed to attract, retain, and satisfy the gambling customer.

Lifestyles of Dealers

The lifestyle of a **dealer** is not well understood by those who don't perform the job. To many outsiders, it seems glamorous. The opportunity to be around the excitement and the money seems attractive. The dealer gets to meet many people throughout the day, and the people bring money and usually energy and excitement with them to the gambling table. This is often perceived as creating a fun, enjoyable, and rewarding job (Figure 8.4).

In contrast, the lifestyle of the typical dealer is almost the opposite. While each is inculcated into the casino culture and well trained in the art of dealing, the requisites of the job mean the dealer becomes virtually an automaton. The game must move along as the casino makes money only when players are betting. Supervisors (pit bosses and shift supervisors) watch dealers to ensure that the pace of the game is steady, with few holdups and delays. Experience has taught the casino how many hands per hour should be dealt based upon the number of players at the blackjack table, or spins of the wheel at roulette, or throws of the dice at craps. Profits are made based upon volume. The more hands that are dealt, the more money is made by the casino. Thus the dealer is under pressure to maintain an expected pace.

FIGURE 8.4 An unhappy gambler.

Source: Image from BigStockPhoto.com.

Maintaining pace is often difficult because some customers want to take more time, to linger over decisions, to socialize with friends, and to drink alcohol. The gambling experience is a social one for most customers. They want to get the most fun out of the experience, and to win money, too! But that winning won't always happen. Given the design of the game, there are winners and losers. Dealers must be ready to handle the angry and disappointed loser, and to support yet control the exuberant winner.

Some gamblers want to chat with the dealer, or to ask advice—which can't be given. The casino can't take the risk that the dealer will give bad advice, or that the outcome will be blamed upon the employee even if good advice is given. So, while some customers want to make the game last longer before they run out of money, to be social, and enjoy themselves, the dealer has to continually press forward to keep the game moving—without displeasing the customers.

The dealer also has to be completely fair in the dealing of every hand. The dealer's actions must follow casino guidelines each and every time. This is to provide customers with a fair and transparent game, but also to protect the game from cheating by customers or employees. The Surveillance department has installed cameras above each table that record each and every action by dealers and customers. Thus, the dealer knows that his/her every move is under constant scrutiny. The pit boss is watching to ensure the game moves along and is dealt accordingly to policy. The customers are watching to ensure fairness. The Surveillance department is watching via overhead cameras. Potentially, shift supervisors and undercover security employees posing as customers are also watching. The dealer is therefore pressured to perform the task of dealing in a consistent manner, time after time after time.

FIGURE 8.5   Friends having fun at the blackjack table.

Source: Image from BigStockPhoto.com.

This constant activity of dealing in a uniform manner, over and over, and doing so at a regular pace, and managing customer interactions at the table help to create the job condition of behaving as an automaton. The dealer almost becomes robotic in his/her actions. These conditions take a toll on the employee. Because of this, most dealers deal only for one hour, and then take a 20-minute break (Figure 8.5).

Dealers also have to contend with customer personalities and superstitions. Some players feel "lucky" with a certain dealer, and will follow the dealer as he/she is assigned different tables. Other players attach blame to a specific dealer, or label one as "unlucky" and so avoid that dealer, sometimes making a public fuss about it. It is difficult for dealers to take this treatment at times, especially when the dealer is under pressure to keep the game rolling, and to patiently and quietly take such mild abuse from unhappy gamblers. The regular break schedule helps the casino deal with these situations. Having the dealer move to the back-of-the-house for a break, and to remove the dealer from the sight of the customer, is often a solution that resolves the problem. In more extreme cases, the pit boss or the shift supervisor intervenes to protect the employee and potentially keep a customer happy.

This superstition about dealers, where some gamblers attribute success or failure to the dealer, is why virtually all casinos have dealers pool their tips into one large fund. It is known that big winners often tip the dealer generously, and those who lose rarely tip the dealer at all. Since the dealer follows protocol in dealing, the outcome of the game isn't dependent upon the dealer at all. Yet, for illogical reasons, some gamblers still insist the dealer is influential. To be fair to all dealers—those who have winners who tip well and those who have losers who blame the dealer, all tips are placed into one large pool that is later shared equally among all dealers. This is also fair to dealers who are assigned shifts during low-volume times where few tips are given.

Each dealer gets a share of the tips based upon the number of hours worked over a period of time, which is usually a month. In this manner, the dealers can focus upon following the dealing rules and not worry about extra efforts to generate individual tips. It also helps the casino control employee cheating. If dealers cannot keep individual tips, then there isn't any incentive to cheat in favor of a customer with the hope of receiving a large tip.

The dealers tend to stick together as a general group, choosing to remain segregated from other types of employees. Their interaction with the games and customers makes them an exclusive group within the larger casino resort. In the larger gaming towns, the dealers often have a community association of their own so that they can share experiences, commiserate with one another about working conditions and difficult customers, and network for opportunities.

The average length of time a person remains a dealer is about five years. With the pressures of constant surveillance, behaving in a robotic fashion day after day, and not earning individual tips for personalized service makers, these employees feel underappreciated. Some do continue to deal for many years, satisfied to remain in the role and content with the job duties. The intangible benefits from being in the heart of the action of a casino, of being around high rollers, newly weds, celebrating friends, big winners, and the allure of potential winnings are often worth it for these long-term employees. Advancement is limited to other table games (roulette, craps, and baccarat) that require a bit more dealing skill, and possibly into supervision. However, the number of entry-level management positions is limited, and many currently in those positions move up only slowly within the organization (Figure 8.6).

In summary, the lifestyle of a dealer is not as glamorous as many outside the industry might think. Dealers must strive to persevere in the face of constant observation by management, surveillance, and customers. The dealers must be able to perform their job in a high-quality manner, following dealing protocol day after day, hour after hour, without mistakes. And their pay is about $30,000–$35,000 per year (salary and tips included), which is less than the median income in America. They work shifts at all hours of the day

FIGURE 8.6   Nevada casino communities are popular locations for informal weddings.

Source: Image from BigStockPhoto.com.

FIGURE 8.7 Upscale boutiques are a convenient place to spend winnings.

Source: Image from BigStockPhoto.com.

and night, both weekdays and weekends. The job has some appeal because it is in the heart of the casino operations where the action happens, but it has limits and restrictions that cause many to leave after a few years. It's a vital job for the casino. Attracting and retaining good dealers is an ongoing challenge for the casino resort. It's a lifestyle that is only for a select few (Figure 8.7).

Lifestyles of Other Casino Employees

There are a number of other employees who work in the casino and are not dealers. Their world is somewhat different than that of the dealers, but it still is unique from workers in other industries. These employees include those who work in the Slots department, the cage and the Accounting department, the administrative departments, the Security department, and those who work as entertainers and shop clerks. While these workers don't have the immediate pressures of the dealers, of being "on" every day, every hour, with customers, they still have the pleasure of working in the exciting gambling environment. They still feel unique and special because of the type of business in which they work. They form an informal fraternity, too, and work the shifts at all hours of the day and night, weekdays, and weekends, as their positions demand.

These workers also share the sense of serving customers. They know that the business revolves around having customers gamble. However, these workers know they do not have the "glamour" jobs in the eyes of the customers. Most of the jobs require few skills and have limited career opportunities. These workers do not have the training required to be dealers, so without that outside education, even those dealing positions are not realistic possibilities for advancement.

The Surveillance department employees have a lifestyle that is distinctly separate from all other employees. They are separated from other departments to ensure they don't form relationships or friendships with other workers that could lead to possible collusion about outright theft or cheating schemes. These workers even use a separate employee entrance to

FIGURE 8.8   Active nightlife activities abound to attract gamblers.

Source: Image from BigStockPhoto.com.

the casino so that they don't mingle with other employees or become known. As their job includes watching employees for cheating, it isn't healthy to have them interacting with those they watch.

Many surveillance employees are former cheats who have been caught, penalized, and are now reformed. Thus, their experience with casinos as gamblers, what they know about what can be done and who might be doing it, helps to set them apart from the rest of the employees. They are specialists in what they do, and have a high value to the casino. They work the shifts as all other workers do, but they do it in seclusion. Thus, their lifestyle is one similar to an undercover police officer. They hide their identities from their coworkers, and they conceal what they do as a profession from everyone. This leads to a separation lifestyle that is certainly unique within a world of unique lifestyles (Figure 8.8).

Conclusion

Everyone who comes into contact with the casino industry ends up feeling different in some fashion. Customers seek fun, excitement, glamour, and the chance to get rich. They often like to show off, to preen and display their fine clothing, and to impress others with their gambling skills and winnings. A visit to a casino resort enables the visitors to adopt a different lifestyle than they have back at home. It enables them to behave differently, to party and celebrate more openly, and to engage in risky gambling activities. It becomes a lifestyle that is practiced only when visiting a casino resort for these visitors know they will eventually return home to a more safe, comfortable, and well-known environment.

Employees of casino resorts develop unique lifestyles, too. The nature of their work and the limited number who do it across the country make them feel involved in something special, something fun and exciting. The reality of the work they do is more mundane, more routine than outsiders might think. But still, these workers are attracted to the work and remain because of the association with the exciting world of casinos. It's enough to keep them interested, and to return to work, day after day after day.

Key Words

Luxor *88*   VIP *89*   Dealer *90*
Excalibur *88*

Review Questions

1. Write an overview of the casino's impact on lifestyles.
2. Describe the impact of casinos on the lifestyles of customers.
3. Explain the unique impact of casinos on the lifestyle of the out-of-town gambler.
4. Detail the unique impact of casinos on the lifestyle of the local gambler.
5. Discuss the impact of casinos on the lifestyles of casino employees.
6. Describe the unique impact of casinos on the lifestyles of dealers.
7. Describe the unique impact of casinos on the lifestyles of other casino employees.

CHAPTER 9

HUMAN RESOURCE ISSUES IN CASINO OPERATIONS

CHRISTOPHER WOODRUFF

Learning Objectives

1. To provide an overview of the Human Resources (HR) department within casino operations
2. To learn about the HR function of finding workers
3. To learn about the HR function of attracting, training, and retaining workers
4. To learn about the HR function of getting workers to the casino
5. To learn about the HR function of getting workers licensed at the casino
6. To understand the function of HR in keeping employees and keeping them happy
7. To understand the role of HR in motivating employees
8. To understand how HR runs employee assistance programs
9. To understand the issue of the effects of secondhand smoke and noise levels on casino employees

Chapter Outline

INTRODUCTION

The Human Resources or Personnel department of a casino has undergone a complete transformation since casinos have been in the United States. For the majority of time, casino employees were just seen as the medium through which the casino offered gaming opportunities to guests. Since the early stages of the modern gaming industry, management has usually treated employees in less than fair terms. Firing without cause, promotion based on "juice" (who you know), and dictator-style management were at one time accepted practices. However, today most casinos are run in a professional corporate manner, and human resources has developed into one of the most important and respected departments of the casino. In this chapter, we examine some of the major human resource issues in casinos that include hiring and retaining workers, employee assistance programs (EAP), employee gambling, alcohol abuse, smoking, depression, exposure to secondhand smoke, and high levels of noise.

THE HUMAN RESOURCES FACTOR

Human Resources (**HR**) plays a vital role in today's casinos. Some of the major duties of a casino HR department are hiring, retaining, and firing of staff; obtaining gaming licenses for those employees who need them; employee orientation training; retention efforts; employee discipline; and offering employee assistance programs. The HR department not only performs these tasks for casino employees, but also provides these activities for the support departments of the casino that usually include hotels, restaurants, and entertainment attractions.

In contrast to many other industries, many people are interested in working in casinos. Typically, the HR department does not have to advertise much to attract applicants. For example, when the Mohegan Sun Casino (Connecticut) first opened, it rented the football stadium at the University of New Haven to accommodate all of the people who responded to their advertisement. The challenge for the HR department is to find qualified workers for the various positions throughout the business, and to work to retain them as long as possible.

The range of jobs within the casino resort varies from the dealers working on the casino floor, to entry-level workers for the restaurants and hotels, and to the staff positions in the support departments where higher education is often a required skill set. The HR department has to be well versed in identifying the diverse skills needed throughout the organization.

Employees working on the casino floor almost always must have some sort of license issued by the state gaming authority. The state is interested in regulating who works in gaming to help ensure a healthy, crime-free business environment. Concerns of the past included racketeering and mob control. The state gaming agencies have been effective in removing such influences. One of the steps in accomplishing this is requiring each casino worker, regardless of position or rank, to be licensed by the state.

For example, in the state of Nevada, only employees working on the casino floor itself and in the ranks of management are required to be licensed. Workers in the restaurants, hotels, shops, entertainment, and so on, need not have licenses. In contrast, at the other end of the spectrum, the state of New Jersey requires that all employees who work for the casino organization, regardless of duties or position, must be licensed. Many other

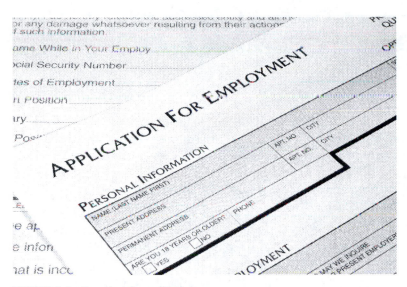

FIGURE 9.1 Sample job application.

Source: Image from BigStockPhoto.com.

states have licensing variations with requirements between these two extremes. Thus, a first requirement of the HR department is to ensure that prospective employees can obtain the appropriate state license. Without the state license, an employee is not permitted to work in the casino (Figure 9.1).

Finding Workers

The next important step for the HR department is to find workers for the casino who have proper dealer training. The casinos wish to hire dealers who have completed dealer's school and are well versed in the proper procedures for dealing the major casino games. In most gaming communities, a number of small businesses have opened that provide dealer training to people who want to work in this industry. Dealer applicants are expected to complete a recognized "dealer training" program prior to applying for work at the casino.

The requirements of the state for licensing combined with the generally large pool of people who want to work in casinos has helped create this small cottage industry of dealer-training schools. It has enabled the casino to essentially transfer a large segment of dealer employee training to the shoulders of the applicant. While each casino still has to provide some training to dealers to orient them to its unique policies and procedures, hiring dealers who have had outside training helps the casino reduce its cost and training effort.

Retaining dealers is a challenge for the HR department. The job of dealer is one that has a very strict routine. Dealers must deal the cards or operate the table game in a controlled, consistent manner. Customers expect fairness and do not want the dealers to unfairly influence the game. Therefore, the dealers must perform in a mechanical manner to achieve the needed consistency. The job becomes highly repetitive. Dealers tire easily and typically work for one hour, take a 20-minute break, and then return to deal again for another hour. Over time, the job of dealing becomes boring to many dealers. In general, the average tenure of a dealer is about five years. The HR department works with these dealers to retain as many as they can for as long as they can.

FIGURE 9.2 New dealers are trained to deal according to specific and strict procedures.

Source: Image from BigStockPhoto.com.

Dealers have some advancement opportunities. Dealing blackjack is the entry-level dealing position, so promotion to more complex games is possible. Dealers need different skills for operating a roulette game or helping to run a craps table (Figure 9.2). Thus, dealers can work to improve their skills and move into more desirable dealer positions. A few dealers do make the transition from dealing into supervision and management. As each pit has a pit boss and shift supervisor, candidates are often selected from among the dealers.

Attracting, Training, and Retaining Workers

The HR department also attracts, trains, and works to retain workers in the casino restaurants and hotels. The skills needed for many of these positions are entry level, requiring basic knowledge of food service or hygiene. The training for food service workers (waitstaff, cooks, other kitchen help, etc.) is fairly straightforward. Experienced workers from traditional restaurants easily make the transition into the casino food service environment. Thus, the HR department views these skilled food service workers as a preferred target.

Workers for the hotel range from housekeepers (room cleaners) to desk clerks to office support staff. Every position held in a traditional hotel is needed in a casino hotel. The skill sets are the same in both environments. Thus, the HR department seeks new employees who have prior experience working in hotels.

Not all applicants to the casino, however, want entry-level positions such as housekeepers. The HR department has the same challenges in filling some of these positions as traditional hotels. Occasionally, incentives are sometimes needed to attract sufficient quantities of workers for these positions.

The staffing of support departments is also the responsibility of the HR department. Positions in marketing, accounting and finance, general management, and the top management team are needed as existing employees leave the organization and vacancies occur. Working with each department, the HR department identifies the skills and abilities needed for each position and works to fill each vacancy.

Getting Employees There

Perhaps the most obvious duty of an HR department is to hire employees. However, that is not as easy as it sounds. Some new casinos have to hire thousands of people at one time to staff for their opening. They not only have to find these people, but interview many more, sometimes interviewing three or more applicants for every position filled! Once hired, the HR department must then train and orientate the new employees, and help them to obtain gaming licenses. In fact, more than 26,000 people applied for 2,000 jobs at a casino in Detroit, Michigan—all 26,000 had to be screened, and then over 7,000 interviews were conducted! When the Mirage Hotel and Casino first opened in Las Vegas, more than 53,000 people applied for over 5,600 positions. These daunting numbers created a monumental task for its HR department: Hire just the right person for the right job (Figure 9.3).

Getting Employees Licensed

Employee licensing requirements vary by state. On one end of the spectrum is New Jersey, with its highly restrictive approach where everyone working in the entire resort complex, regardless of work duties and proximity to gambling, must be licensed. On the other end

FIGURE 9.3 Slot employees would service machines such as these found inside Harrah's Casino in Atlantic City, New Jersey.

Source: Rudi Von Briel/PhotoEdit Inc.

is the more lax approach in Nevada, where only those who work on the casino floor itself are required to be licensed. The following is a typical example of what you have to do to get a gaming license to work in a casino (Table 9.1).

TABLE 9.1   A Licensing Example from the Michigan Gaming Control Board (MGCB)

CASINO EMPLOYEES/OCCUPATIONAL LICENSES

Many casino employees and employees of companies that supply goods and services to casinos are required to be licensed by the MGCB in accordance with Michigan law. The following is provided as a general reference to help you better understand MGCB licensing requirements and procedures.

- You must be at least 21 years old to work in any gaming function (at least 18 years old if working in a nongaming function).
- The first step in applying for an occupational license is to contact the casino's or supplier company's Human Resources department (or similarly designated office).
- If you are hired, or if the casino/supplier company extends to you an invitation of employment, you will be required to complete an application for submission to the MGCB. As part of the application process, you will be photographed and fingerprinted. The casino/supplier will have more information regarding this procedure. Upon receipt of the application and fee, the MGCB will conduct a background investigation of each applicant and will determine if an occupational license will be issued. Your application must be accompanied by an application fee (see the Fee Schedule later).

Note: The MGCB will not process an application for an occupational license without a written statement from the casino/supplier that you have been hired, or that the casino/supplier intends to hire you. For this reason, you must first apply to the casino/supplier Human Resources department.

LEVELS OF MGCB OCCUPATIONAL LICENSES

There are three Levels of MGCB occupational licenses.

LEVEL ONE—Managers, supervisors, or other key employees. People who have authority to develop or administer policy, long-range plans, or to make discretionary decisions regulating gaming operations; people responsible for major sections within the casino or its property, even if no gaming is conducted in the area (such as a hotel or restaurant). Also, some employees of suppliers will be required to be licensed.

- Level One examples (casino managers/supervisor) of:
  - Accountants, cashiers, and other fiscal staff
  - Casino entertainment
  - Casino food and beverage service
  - Casino games
  - Casino hotel
  - Casino Human Resources department
  - Casino restaurant
  - Slot machine/bill-changer repair and maintenance
  - Some employees of suppliers
  - Surveillance/security investigations
  - Table games
  - Supplier managers/supplier supervisors of repair or maintenance staffs who service slot machines, bill changers, and so on
  - Any person who is required to hold a Level One license

LEVEL TWO—Employees who operate or maintain casino games, or who come in contact with gaming money, chips, tokens, credit slips, and so on, but who are not supervisors.

- Level Two examples (casino employees):
  - Accountants and financial controllers
  - Card dealers and other table game workers
  - Cashiers
  - Computer data input staff and technicians
  - Marketing staff/promotion staff of casino gaming
  - Money changers
  - Money transfer workers
  - Security guards who work in restricted areas of the casino or provide physical security in the casino
  - Slot machine technicians and repair staff
  - Supplier examples:
    - Repair and maintenance of slot machines
    - Repair or maintenance of close circuit TV systems
    - Maintenance of computer hardware

LEVEL THREE—Employees who work in an area where gaming is conducted, or in areas that directly affect gaming, but do not conduct the games or come in contact with gaming money, chips, tokens, credit slips, and so on.

- Level Three examples (casino or supplier):
  - Housekeepers in casino area
  - Nongaming maintenance staff in casino area
  - Waiters/waitresses in casino area
  - Security guards/security workers (whether or not in uniform)

FEES

The MGCB requires a nonrefundable application fee from each applicant to be submitted with the application. Application fees are based on the level of the occupational license. The MGCB also requires a license fee upon issuance of a license and upon any renewal. Occupational licenses are valid for two years, and may be renewed by the MGCB.

Level of Occupational License	Application Fee (nonrefundable)	License Fee
Level One	$500	$250
Level Two	$100	$100
Level Three	$ 50	$ 50

JOBS THAT DO NOT REQUIRE A LICENSE

Generally, employees who do *not* work in areas where gaming is conducted, or do *not* work with money, chips or tokens, are *not* required to be licensed.

- Examples:
  - Coat-check staff
  - Cooks
  - General laborers

(*continued*)

TABLE 9.1   A Licensing Example from the Michigan Gaming Control Board (MGCB) (*continued*)

- General office staff
- Groundskeepers
- Hotel reservation clerks
- Housekeeping/maintenance staff
- Parking lot attendants
- Public relations staff
- Receptionists
- Sales clerks
- Telephone operators
- Wait staff

Note: The MGCB will deny issuing an occupational license if you have been convicted of:

- Any felony
- A misdemeanor involving gambling, theft, dishonesty, or fraud
- You may also be denied a license if the MGCB determines that you are not suitable for such license due to your integrity, moral character, or reputation

The MGCB is assisted by the Michigan Attorney General and Michigan State Police in conducting background investigations. In addition, casinos may have their own requirements for employment, such as submitting to a test for illegal drugs.

TIMEFRAME

The MGCB makes every effort to handle each application in the most expeditious manner possible. However, the MGCB takes whatever time necessary to conduct a thorough background investigation. Background investigations may take several weeks depending on the level of license required and the complexity of the investigation.

TEMPORARY OCCUPATIONAL LICENSES

Temporary occupational licenses enable an employee to begin work with a casino/supplier pending completion of the background investigation by the MGCB. The MGCB may issue a temporary occupational license if a preliminary review of the application and a computerized criminal history check do not indicate any discrepancies that could result in denial. Temporary occupational licenses are valid for 90 days from the date of issue and may be renewed by the MGCB if no disqualifying information is revealed during the investigation. Persons denied a license by the MGCB may request a hearing. If denial is upheld, you may appeal to a circuit court.

It is important to note that in most cases an HR department has to hire you first, or sign a commitment to hire form, before a gaming license application can be submitted. This is a very long process that has to be replicated perhaps thousands of times, depending on the size of the casino! Your employment is contingent upon successful licensing by the state. Without the license, the casino is forbidden to hire you.

KEEPING EMPLOYEES AND KEEPING THEM HAPPY

HR is also very interested in retaining the employees they have. As mentioned earlier, attrition will always happen in a casino as in any other business, but since a casino employs so many people, and with the average recruiting and training cost of an employee sometimes exceeding $10,000 per worker, casinos are concerned now more than ever with keeping the trained employees that they have.

While employee pay and benefits will always be the leading reasons employees either stay or go, casino HR departments are looking at the other reasons, such as the way employees are treated by their supervisors, and job enjoyment, that affect employee satisfaction. Some ideas HR departments have implemented to help with employee retention include:

- Providing higher pay and/or better benefits than other employers.
- Offering clear career-path plans that encourage employees to stay and grow with the company.
- Proper and continuous training.
- Empowering employees, or giving them a say in handling guest situations.
- Listening to employee ideas for department betterment.
- Treating the employee right, since this is a direct pipeline to treating casino guests right.
- Making sure the right person is hired for the right job in the first place.

MOTIVATING YOUR EMPLOYEES

Employee motivation is also a key to keeping your employees happy. Employee motivation simply means doing things that motivate your employees. The goal is to have employees who want to do well in their jobs and to have them want to come to work each day. It is important to remember that every employee is motivated; he/she is just motivated by different things. What managers can do is to learn what motivates different employees and make sure they offer the appropriate incentives when feasible. Two keys to properly motivating employees are reducing the number of rules you have, and making them very clear by publishing them, and following them (Table 9.2).

TABLE 9.2   Top Ten Ways to Motivate Your Employees

Top Ten Ways to Motivate Your Employees
10. Train your employees in new areas or teach them new skills
9. Recognize the accomplishments of your employees
8. Get your employees involved in decision making (empower your employees)
7. Keep your employees informed of decisions affecting their jobs
6. Respect your employees
5. Provide feedback to your employees on how they are performing
4. Trust your employees
3. Tell your employees you appreciate them
2. Thank your employees for a job well done
1. Find out what motivates your employees

FIGURE 9.4   Typical entertainment position available for stage dancers.

EMPLOYEE ASSISTANCE PROGRAMS

An important part of keeping your employees healthy is offering employee assistance programs (**EAP**). Some examples are stop smoking programs, healthy living programs, and personal financial management advice. Other nontraditional programs include helping an unemployed family member get a job and day care services for both children and dependent adults. The important logic with EAPs is that an employee who is healthy and happy at home will perform the duties of his/her job better. Another benefit of an EAP is that it shows your employees that you care about their well-being. This investment in employees does help to retain vital workers (Figure 9.4).

OTHER HUMAN RESOURCE ISSUES IN CASINOS

While all businesses have problem employees, a Harvard Medical School study showed that casinos have a higher likelihood of having employees involved in a number of problem areas. These areas include:

- Pathological gambling behavior
- Smoking

- Problem alcohol use
- Depression
- Exposure to secondhand smoke
- Exposure to high noise levels

These are important concerns for any worker but the care and treatment of most of them is usually beyond the abilities of the casino HR department. The EAPs can offer employees referrals to outside assistance programs such as Gambler's Anonymous or Alcoholics Anonymous, if needed to deal with gambling, smoking, drug, and alcohol abuse. Counseling can be arranged for employees dealing with depression. The key is for employees to be aware of such assistance, and for the casino to provide it in a confidential and supportive manner.

EFFECTS OF SECONDHAND SMOKE AND NOISE ON CASINO EMPLOYEES

Some of the problem areas are potentially within the scope of the casino. This includes exposure to **secondhand smoke** and high noise levels. Twenty-seven states plus Washington D.C. have enacted 100% smoke-free gambling. The whole argument with providing a smoke-free business is that even if you do not smoke, you can be harmed by the cigarette and cigar smoke of others. The same does not apply to drinking alcohol in that drinking has no direct affect on those who are around a drinker. Since employees are always subjected to secondhand smoke in those casinos that allow smoking, it has become a big issue with many HR departments. Some employees have sued employers for exposing them to secondhand smoke and forcing them to work in a hazardous environment.

Many states and towns have passed nonsmoking laws for businesses; however, many times casinos, hotels, and restaurants are exempt from these laws. The reason is that these businesses have convinced lawmakers that their businesses would be greatly harmed if smoking bans were implemented since many people smoke in restaurants, hotels, and casinos. In fact, a smoking ban at the Casino Windsor caused 300 workers and 32 salaried staff members to be laid off within a month of the ban due to decreasing revenues directly related to the smoking ban.[1] This debate will not go away and may be solved only if an employee wins a lawsuit against a casino and then wins monetary damages from the casino. The casinos are being forced to choose between the health and safety of their employees or staying profitable.

The National Institute for Occupational Safety and Health **(NIOSH)** received a complaint from the employees of Spirit Mountain Casino saying that the noise generated by the slot machines was causing them to lose their hearing. NIOSH conducted decibel tests at the casino and reported that no occupational exposure to noise would harm the hearing of employees at Spirit Mountain Casino. While there was no medical damage done to employees, HR departments should still be aware of the risk of high noise levels and make sure their employees are exposed only to noise levels within the acceptable range for health and safety (Figure 9.5).

FIGURE 9.5   Physical plant employees care for the grounds and exhibits such as these fountains at the Bellagio.

Conclusion

While some executives in the casino industry still see the HR department as a "necessary evil," most now see how important the HR department is in directly affecting the profits of the casino. Since most managers agree that "employees treat the guest as well as they are treated" or "our reputation is established by our employees," the HR department has been transformed into a major force in the success of the overall casino. It plays a major role in the recruitment of trained workers, and in retaining them. Given the highly competitive nature of the casino industry at this time and the high cost of replacing workers, retaining trained employees is a key goal for most organizations. The HR department also plays a vital role in the ongoing satisfaction of employees. Offering additional training, engaging in career planning, providing support for personal and professional problems through EAPs, and so on are many of the steps the HR department can undertake to help satisfy and motivate workers. Without an effective HR department, the burden of operating a successful casino would be much more difficult.

Key Words

HR *98*

MGCB *102*

EAP *106*

Secondhand smoke *107*

NIOSH *107*

Review Questions

1. Write an overview of the HR department within casino operations.
2. Describe the HR function of finding workers.
3. Describe the HR function of attracting, training, and retaining workers.
4. Explain the HR function of getting workers to the casino.

5. Explain the HR function of getting workers licensed at the casino.
6. Detail the function of HR in keeping employees and keeping them happy.
7. Explain the role of HR in motivating employees.
8. Explain how HR's can run EAP.
9. Discuss the issue of the effects of secondhand smoke and noise levels on casino employees.

Bibliography

NIOSH. HETA # 2003-0157-2934. Spring Mountain Casino, April 2004.

Shaffer, H. "Gambling, Drinking, Smoking, and other Health Risks Among Casino Employees." *American Journal of Industrial Medicine* 36, no. 3 (2008).

Smith, J. "Job Hopefuls Flock to MGM." *The Detroit News*, Wednesday March 28, 2007.

Trout, D. "Exposure of Casino Employees to Environmental Tobacco Smoke." *Journal of Occupational & Environmental Medicine* 40, no 3 (1998), 270–276.

Endnote

1. WLNS, Lansing (2006). *Smoking Ban Causing 300 to Be Laid Off at Casino Windsor*. Retrieved May 2, 2008, from http://www.wlns.com/global/story.asp?s=8945.

CHAPTER 10

RESPONSIBLE GAMBLING AND ADDICTIVE BEHAVIORS

CHRIS ROBERTS AND MARYANN CONRAD

Learning Objectives

1. To provide an overview of the issues of responsible gambling and addictive behaviors
2. To learn the differences between problem gambling and pathological gambling
3. To understand the prevalence of problem and pathological gambling in the general population
4. To understand the contrasting attitudes and beliefs of gamblers and nongamblers
5. To learn about gambling attitudes and beliefs in general
6. To learn the various levels of gambling frequencies, activities, expenditures, and behaviors
7. To learn the definition and features of responsible gambling
8. To learn of programs to foster responsible gambling

Chapter Outline

INTRODUCTION

Gambling and risk taking have been part of human culture since the beginning of recorded history. Early accounts of gambling apparatus date back many centuries. For example, ivory dice made sometime before 1500 B.C.E. have been recovered from Egyptian tombs. The Chinese, Japanese, Greeks, and Romans were also known to practice games of skill and chance for amusement as early as 2300 B.C.E. Both Native American and European colonists' history and culture of gambling shaped early American views and practices. Native Americans, believing gods determined their luck and chance, developed games and language related to gambling, while the British colonization of America was partly financed through various lottery game proceeds beginning in the early seventeenth century. During the Georgian era in England, lotteries were viewed as a popular form of taxation, thereby becoming popular in America as European settlers arrived here. The American Revolutionary War was funded, in part, by lotteries. American societal standards of tolerance and acceptance and laws related to gambling have swung back and forth over time from prohibition to regulation. Parallel to the expansion and growth of the gaming industry in the late twentieth and early twenty-first centuries has been the growing awareness of and attention to the issue of problem and pathological gambling.

Recurring accounts of gamblers suffering losses are recorded from early times, with the behavior labeled as an addiction. Descriptions of what is now clinically described as pathological gambling have been noted in historical accounts of many world cultures. Psychoanalysts first became interested in gambling as a disorder in the first half of the twentieth century. Freud, for example, believed gambling was an addiction and that the gambler gambled not for the money but for what is known today as "the action."

As gambling in the United States expanded after its legalization in the 1930s, problems associated with it began to garner greater attention, exemplified by the first meeting of **Gambler's Anonymous**, the 12-step self-help fellowship, that took place in 1957. Gambler's Anonymous' well-known screening questions became the standard used in measuring compulsive gambling behavior and served as the basis for modern classification systems that determine the seriousness of an individual's gambling problem by focusing on consequences of the gambling behavior (Figure 10.1).

PROBLEM GAMBLING VERSUS PATHOLOGICAL GAMBLING

The term "problem gambling" is often used to describe both the pathological and the problem gambler, yet there exists a distinction between the two. Not all problem gamblers are pathological gamblers, but all pathological gamblers are considered to be problem gamblers. **Pathological gambling**, often thought of as "compulsive" gambling, is not clinically considered to be a compulsive behavior. The clinical classification of pathological gambling is "impulse control disorder." There are ten criteria used to diagnose the behavior. **Problem gamblers** are thought to suffer from a broad range of harmful consequences as a result of their gambling but fall below the line of at least five of the ten criteria used in diagnosing pathological gambling. "At-risk" gamblers are defined as those who meet one or two of the ten criteria (Table 10.1). These gamblers are at higher risk to develop problems with gambling, but also may gamble recreationally for their entire lives without ever suffering any ill consequences.

Pathological gambling is different from the social and recreational gambling of most adults. Social or recreational players gamble for entertainment, typically do not risk more

FIGURE 10.1   Losing is never fun.

Source: Image from BigStockPhoto.com.

TABLE 10.1   *DSM-IV* Diagnostic Criteria

A. Persistent and recurrent maladaptive gambling behavior as indicated by at least five of the following:
1. Is preoccupied with gambling (e.g., preoccupied with reliving past gambling experiences, handicapping or planning the next venture, or thinking of ways to get money with which to gamble)
2. Needs to gamble with increasing amounts of money in order to achieve the desired excitement
3. Has repeated unsuccessful efforts to control, cut back, or stop gambling
4. Is restless or irritable when attempting to cut down or stop gambling
5. Gambles as a way of escaping from problems or of relieving a dysphoric mood (e.g., feelings of helplessness, guilt, anxiety, depression)
6. After losing money gambling, often returns another day in order to get even ("chasing" one's losses)
7. Lies to family members, therapists, or others to conceal the extent of involvement with gambling
8. Has committed illegal acts, such as forgery, fraud theft, or embezzlement, in order to finance gambling
9. Has jeopardized or lost a significant relationship, job, or educational career opportunity because of gambling
10. Relies on others to provide money to relieve a desperate financial situation caused by gambling

B. The gambling behavior is not better accounted for by a Manic Episode.

Source: American Psychiatric Association (1994), *Diagnostic and Statistical Manual of Mental Disorders, Fourth Edition.*

FIGURE 10.2   Example of an extreme bet a problem gambler might make.

Source: Image from BigStockPhoto.com.

than they are able to afford, and have little preoccupation with gambling. According to the National Council on Problem Gambling (**NCPG**),[1] key features of problem and pathological gambling include "increasing preoccupation with gambling, the need to bet more money more frequently, 'chasing' losses, and loss of control by continuation of the gambling behavior in spite of mounting, serious, negative consequences." These negative consequences can include crime, financial debt and bankruptcies, loss of career, homelessness, damaged family and personal relationships, and even suicide. It is estimated that as many as 20% of these gamblers will attempt suicide. Two-thirds of those seeking help have engaged in criminal activity in support of their gambling habit (Figure 10.2).

PREVALENCE IN THE GENERAL POPULATION

Concurrent with the increase in the legalization of gambling, prevalence studies measuring pathological and problem gambling began in the 1970s. Three large-scale studies have been undertaken to examine this issue. In 1976, a national study undertaken by the University of Michigan Survey Research Center[2] concentrated on assessing adult American gambling activities and attitudes towards gambling. From the responses, 0.77% (less than 1%) of the national sample could be classified as a "probable compulsive gambler" while 2.33% fell into the "potential compulsive gambler" category. Caution was advised, however, in interpreting the results, as the study was not clear in distinguishing compulsive gambling from other possible disorders (Figure 10.3).

In the majority of cases, most pathological gamblers had more than one compulsive disorder (**comorbidity**) like with alcohol or drugs. It is suggested that one of the possible reasons is that gamblers have an addictive personality such as the Type A personality. These are people who are driven to do things over and above the normal person's actions like work excessively. Another reason is that people get hooked on the chemical adrenaline rush that occurs from the excitement of winning. These types of people are risk takers who have the need to test the limits of their boundaries in order to repeat the chemical high they receive such as bungee jumpers. Sometimes veterans from wars who have repeatedly

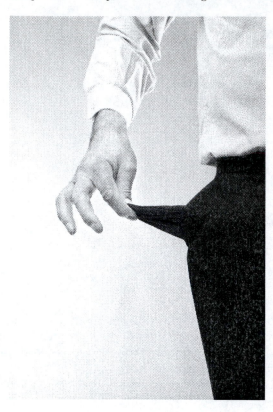

FIGURE 10.3 Gamblers who spend it all may be potential problem or pathological gamblers.

Source: Image from BigStockPhoto.com.

been on the edge of their endurance come home with a need for adrenaline rushes. With pathological gamblers, many have a similar cycle: they are new to gambling; they hit big early in their careers; and then they chase "losses." This means that they bet $1. If they lose they bet $2, and so on.

In 1997, a large-scale study was undertaken to estimate the prevalence of pathological and problem gambling in the United States and Canada (Harvard Meta-Analysis).[3] Although no significant overall difference was found between gamblers in the United States and Canada, significant differences were found among four population segments. A combined total of 5.45% of adults was estimated to fall into problem or pathological gambling at some point during their lifetimes. Prevalence rates for youth, college students, and the prison/treatment populations, however, were found to be substantially higher. The study also indicated that prevalence estimates were found to have increased between the 1970s and 1990s, indicating that as gambling became more socially acceptable and accessible over those two decades, more people gambled, and problem gambling behavior increased.

In 1999, another study conducted by the National Research Council indicated that 1.5% of adults in the United States, at some point in their lives, have been pathological or compulsive gamblers and that in any given year 0.9% (less than 1%) of adults in the United States are pathological gamblers. Rates of pathological gambling among adolescents and college students have been consistently higher than that of adults. Estimates of the level of lifetime problem gambling among gambling-addicted adolescents is 2.9% while gambling-addicted college students have an average estimate of lifetime problem gambling of 5%.

FIGURE 10.4 The ease of access to Internet-based casinos creates issues for underage and problem gamblers.

Source: Image from BigStockPhoto.com.

The research data suggests that the prevalence of problem and pathological gambling has increased over the past few decades, and that the severity of problem gambling is increasing. Furthermore, the proportion of individuals who score at the higher end of the problem gambling spectrum is growing. Although it is possible that problem/pathological gambling will continue to increase, it is also possible that the prevalence rates will remain constant or even diminish. After people have gained adequate experience with gambling activities, they may begin to adapt to the experience and protect themselves from the possibilities of the harmful consequences of the behavior (Figure 10.4).

ATTITUDES AND BELIEFS: GAMBLERS VERSUS NONGAMBLERS

In order to assess gamblers, their behaviors, and their potential for problems, it is important to find out who these gamblers are and what their actions are outside gambling regarding money and planning. From two reports, the National Profile Study (Roper Reports GfK NOP) and the U.S. Gaming Panel (TNS) which are used by the U.S. Census population data,[4] many findings about the national population can be assessed. In terms of personal finances, more gamblers (23%) increased their savings in the past year than nongamblers (16%). In fact, 28% of gamblers put away money for the future in the previous year compared to 20% nongamblers. When people plan to invest their money, gamblers consider themselves to be intermediate to knowledgeable investors (43%) over nongamblers (33%). Generally gamblers are more confident about making financial decisions, with 78% more optimistic about the future of their personal financial situation than nongamblers (68%). This is why 20% of gamblers are asked their opinion on how to invest by their friends and family, whereas only 12% nongamblers say the same. Overall gamblers are more likely to have planned for their retirement and 65% of them put away money regularly versus 46% of nongamblers. Therefore, it would appear that gamblers are more in control over their assets, their spending patterns, and their future financial needs.

GAMBLING ATTITUDES AND BELIEFS

The Pew Research Center Social Trends Reports[5] examine the behaviors and attitudes of Americans in various aspects of their lives, analyzing changes over time in social behaviors and highlighting differences and similarities between key subgroups in the population. A 2006 Pew Report[6] found that a majority of Americans approve of most forms of legalized gambling, where only 28% of participants stated that it is morally wrong to gamble. The report further found that attitudes about gambling are strongly correlated with one's own gambling behavior; one's experiences with problem gambling in the family; and one's level of religious adherence. Those who are less supportive are also those who do not gamble, those who report gambling-related family dysfunction, women, older adults (65 years and older), the less educated, the less affluent, and those who frequently attend church. The youngest subgroup (18–29 years) had the lowest percentage (26%) rejecting the notion that gambling is immoral.

Since 1989 there has been a negative turn in attitudes toward some types of gambling in all demographic groups surveyed (e.g., lotteries: 78% to 71% approval rating, bingo for cash: 75% to 66% approval rating). The approval ratings for casino gambling and off-track betting on horse races approval dropped slightly (54% to 51% and 54% to 50%, respectively) while betting on pro sports remained stable (42% approval rating). The decreases are supposedly driven by the concern that people are gambling too much, rather than gambling is immoral—formerly a more commonly held view. Seventy percent of Americans say that legalized gambling encourages people to gamble more than they can afford, up eight points from a similar survey conducted in 1989. All major demographic groups report this increase, with the exception of the 18- to 29-year-olds who remained stable in their attitudes.

On the other hand, in 2008 consider that 84% of gamblers *always* set a budget before they started to gamble with 6% *usually* setting a budget, and 5% *sometimes*. Only 4% *never* set a budget ahead of time. Out of the 95% of people who set budgets at least sometimes, 25% set a limit of $100–$199 and 50% set their spending at less than $100.[7]

GAMBLING FREQUENCIES, ACTIVITIES, EXPENDITURES, AND BEHAVIORS

Two-thirds (67%) of the participants in the 2006 Pew survey stated they had placed a bet within the past 12 months, down slightly from 71% who reported gambling within the past 12 months in a 1989 Gallup survey. Although certain types of gambling activities have declined in frequency, others forms of gambling, such as casino and slot machines, have become more popular. Seven in ten gamblers reported gambling for enjoyment while two in ten report gambling to make money.

Online gambling, a more recent form of wagering, is growing in popularity with between 2% and 4% of the American public participating in 2007. Although still a small number, both sources report this percentage has doubled, from Pew's previous 1996 survey and the American Gaming Association (AGA) report from 2005, signaling an increase in this form of gambling. The 2006 Pew survey also reports that playing a state lottery

TABLE 10.2 Reported Wins/Losses by Gamblers in 2006

Single-Day Win/Loss	Largest Win	Largest Loss
Overall mean	$1,049	$492
Overall median	$ 100	$ 25
Men	$1,536	Not reported
Women	$ 537	Not reported

Based on 1,473 people who gambled in the past year (at the time of the study).

Source: Pew Research Center, 2006.

continues to be the most popular gambling activity with over half (52%) of the American adult population participating within the past 12 months; casino visitation was second at 29%; and slot play next at 24%.

Self-reported wins and losses differed by age with nearly half (49%) of all 18 to 29-year-old gamblers reporting to be ahead for the year; more than double the percentage of all gamblers over 65 who report to be ahead (23%). This suggests that younger players tend to "forget" their losses and bolster their winnings more than older players. The younger group also reported the greatest satisfaction in winning. Gamblers in the Pew survey in 2006 report by a ratio of nearly two-to-one that they are behind in winnings for the year, however their self-reported best and worst days tell a different story (Table 10.2). The survey states the inconsistency can be explained either by gamblers occasionally winning big sums and frequently losing small sums and/or by human memory remembering the best days more vividly than the losing ones. For more detailed information on human perceptions about gambling, read the chapter "Consumer Behavior" in *Casino Marketing: Theories and Applications* the marketing book from this series.

RESPONSIBLE GAMBLING

The gaming industry has radically shifted its perspective of this issue from that of 40 years ago. Since the early 1980s, Harrah's Entertainment, Inc. has promoted responsible gaming when a group of employees formed a task force to study the issue of problem gaming. After months of research, the task force developed the industry's first initiative to help employees, guests, and the public understand the importance of responsible gaming and the prevention of underage gambling.[8] Fifteen years later in 1995, AGA was formed to represent the industry in legislative and public forums. Its primary goal is to educate the general public and to advocate for industry members. The members of this association include casino resorts, equipment manufacturers, vendors, and suppliers in the gaming industry. This association has become the most powerful speaker for the industry to the public and in Washington lobbying for the rights of the industry. During this inception period, Harrah's helped fund the creation and start-up of the first national helpline (1-800-522-4700) for problem gambling. Harrah's continue to fund the counselors and provide confidential counseling assistance to their own employees through an employee assistance program. A year later, Boyd Gaming provided the start-up funds for the creation of the first and only national program of its kind, the National Center for Responsible Gaming (**NCRG**) and made a ten-year pledge of $875,000. This national organization was established exclusively to fund peer-reviewed scientific research on underage, problem, and pathological gambling. They also fund efforts to develop effective methods of treatment, and broad efforts to educate the general public about responsible gaming.

Today, the gaming industry is very involved in the issue of responsible gambling. No longer do casino employees ignore individuals exhibiting gambling problems. Instead, they are trained to watch for symptoms and to take action when appropriate. These actions range from simply providing customers with information and possible sources for assistance, to working with management to intervene more aggressively when necessary. Sometimes, employees will take up a collection to provide a gambler with bus fare to return home. To support this approach, casino resorts actively train employees about responsible gambling and offer periodic refresher courses to keep the concepts in the forefront of everyone's awareness. In addition, IGT, an international gaming manufacturing company, created the position for the only director of responsible gaming in the gaming manufacturing industry. This person is dedicated to implementing the corporate responsible gaming program.

PROGRAMS TO FOSTER RESPONSIBLE GAMBLING

AGA developed an aggressive publication education program to increase awareness of problem gambling and to promote responsible gaming practices. Several casino firms had already started similar programs. The association built upon those efforts to create a national effort. For example, Harrah's Entertainment created Operation Bet Smart and Project 21, which are designed to prepare casino employees to handle customers with gambling problems. Operation Bet Smart is designed to give employees information about company gaming policies and tactics to use to help others when they recognize a critical situation. The program's overall goal is to make employees more aware of the issues of problem gambling and to increase each employee's comfort level in handling them. Within the casinos, they provide responsible gaming signage on the floor and back of the house as well as on brochures, telephone hold messages, player cards, and hotel directories (Figure 10.5).

Project 21 is designed to increase awareness of underage gambling and its consequences. Beyond educating employees, both programs also include the creation of public service announcements and the publication of materials for public education. Also, information is available on front- and back-of-the-house signage. The program has been so successful that Harrah's now licenses it to other casinos. In addition, Harrah's created an Unattended Children Policy to encourage parents not to leave their children unattended at properties. Then it also trains employees on the proper way to approach an unattended child. Another program that most casinos have adopted is the self-restriction/self exclusion. This program allows a person to request not to receive direct marketing as well as no credit and check cashing privileges. Guests are allowed to request to have all privileges, including play privilege, denied so that they cannot force the casino to let them play in a weak moment.

Since 1996, casino firms, equipment manufacturers, vendors, other nonindustry organizations, and private individuals have donated more than $15 million to the NCRG for its efforts. In 2000, the NCRG funded the creation of the Institute for Research on Pathological Gambling and Related Disorders at the Cambridge Health Alliance, a teaching

FIGURE 10.5 Winning big does create a wonderful feeling of excitement and accomplishment.

Source: Image from BigStockPhoto.com.

affiliate of Harvard Medical School. This institute handles the review, selection, and disbursement of research grants for the NCRG.

In addition to initially funding the NCRG, the AGA also created the **Responsible Gaming National Education Campaign**. Started in 1997, this annual effort enables the industry to spotlight the issues of responsible gaming in both employee training and in public awareness. Some of their brochures over the years include *Responsible Gaming Resource*, the *PROGRESS Kit*, and *Keeping it Fun: A Guide to Responsible Gaming*. To continue the public awareness, AGA developed the Responsible Gaming Education Week. Since 1998, it is held every year during the first week of August and is a coordinated effort on the part of casinos to heighten employee awareness. In 2008, the theme of the week "Let's talk about responsible gaming" was about the role of gaming industry employees as ambassadors for the responsible gaming message and the importance of talking about responsible gaming practices among their colleagues, family members, friends, and casino customers.

Another effort is the Gaming Lecture Series, which is a program that has brought gaming experts to speak about these issues at major gaming destinations since 2001. In 2003, the AGA board of directors created the AGA Code of Conduct for Responsible Gaming, a complete set of guidelines governing employee and customer education, underage gambling, alcohol service, advertising, and research. The purpose is to make responsible gaming an inherent part of daily operations. In 2005, the "Keeping It Fun: A Guide to Responsible Gaming" campaign was first created. The "Keeping It Fun" campaign uses bright orange awareness wristbands that allow gaming industry employees,

FIGURE 10.6 Gambling by yourself can be a very lonely experience.

Source: Image from BigStockPhoto.com.

casino patrons, and the public to show their support for the importance of responsible gaming awareness. More than 285,000 wristbands were sold within the year. The proceeds ($115,000) from the wristbands were donated to the NCRG.[9]

Harrah's was the first to develop a broadcast advertising campaign focused specifically on responsible gaming. Ads featured then-CEO Gary Lovement explaining the importance of responsible gaming and how responsible gaming is an important part of their Code of Commitment. Shortly after, AGA introduced its first responsible gaming public service announcements (PSAs) on the Travel Channel. These included tips on how to gamble responsibly and reminded players, "When you play for fun, you've already won." Print editions that member companies could customize for their use followed up this campaign (Figure 10.6).

Conclusion

Over the past three decades the gaming industry has expanded at unprecedented rates, growing tenfold since the mid 1970s. As this growth has happened, the gaming industry has shifted its position from one of letting each gambler handle his or her own gambling issues to one of responsible gambling. Employees are regularly trained to identify a gambler in trouble and to offer information and other aid to help. The industry has formed and supports several associations and foundations whose primary purposes include educating and increasing awareness about problem gambling.

Concurrently with this growth and development, these foundations have funded a number of research studies to explore problem gambling. Several tools and diagnostic measures have been developed to screen for problem and pathological behavior. In addition, most of the gaming organizations also belong to, and work with the NCPG to see how they can help. As a result, Harrah's was awarded the National Council's first corporate award, which recognized Harrah's for its proactive efforts on responsible gaming. However, there still remains a lack of understanding, effective assessment tools, and preventative and educational programs designed for special segments of the population, including the college student population.

Developing a solid understanding of gambling attitudes, behaviors, and awareness, along with motivational factors of gamblers poses numerous challenges for society. This requires that social leaders look at the extent of gambling to determine the types of games most commonly played and to better understand positive and negative attitudes the general public has toward gambling. However, most gaming Web sites begin their commitment to responsible gaming by saying something like, "Penn National Gaming is committed to a policy of Responsible Gaming at all of our gaming and racing facilities. While we recognize that the overwhelming majority of customers participate in our various forms of recreation and amenities in a responsible and rational manner, there is a very small proportion that do not (Figure 10.7). To protect them, and others affected by their behavior, we have established a set of policies and guidelines, modeled after the AGA's "Code of Conduct for Responsible Gaming."[10]

FIGURE 10.7   A blackjack player displays a winning hand.

Source: Image from BigStockPhoto.com.

Key Words

Gambler's anonymous *111*
Pathological gambling *111*
Problem gambling *111*

NCPG *113*
Comorbidity *113*
NCRG *117*

AGA *118*
Responsible Gaming National
    Education Campaign *119*

Review Questions

1. Write an overview of issues of responsible gambling and addictive behaviors.
2. Discuss the differences between problem gambling and pathological gambling.
3. Discuss the prevalence of problem and pathological gambling in the general population.
4. Detail the contrasting attitudes and beliefs of gamblers and nongamblers.
5. Detail and explain gambling attitudes and beliefs in general.
6. Discuss the various levels of gambling frequencies, activities, expenditures, and behaviors.
7. Explain the definition and features of responsible gambling.
8. Discuss the programs available to foster responsible gambling.

Endnotes

1. What is problem gambling? National Council of Problem Gambling. Retrieved June 24, 2008, from http://www.ncpgambling.org/i4a/pages/index.cfm?pageid=3745
2. Surveys of Consumers, University of Michigan (1976). Retrieved June 30, 2008, from http://www.sca.isr.umich.edu/main.php
3. GAO. Impact of gambling: Economic Effects More Measurable Than Social Effects. April 2000, page 45. Retrieved June 30, 2008, from http://books.google.com/books?id=slbR_oH5r08C&pg=PA45&dq=Harvard+Meta-Analysis&sig=ACfU3U0C_pLCAKXaMVrwTCiiLoFAsJWSag#PPP1,M1
4. Profile of the American Casino Gambler: Harrah's Survey 2006. Retrieved June 27, 2008, from http://www.harrahs.com/images/PDFs/Profile_Survey_2006.pdf
5. Pew Research Center Reports: Publications on Social Trends. Retrieved June 30, 2008, from http://pewresearch.org/topics/socialtrends/
6. Pew Research Center Report: Gambling: As the Take Rises, So Does Public Concern. Retrieved June 30, 2008, from http://pewsocialtrends.org/pubs/314/gambling-as-the-take-rises-so-does-public-concern
7. Luntz, Maslansky Strategic Research and Peter D. Hart Research Associates (2008). 2008 AGA Survey of Casino Entertainment. Retrieved June 27, 2008, from http://www.americangaming.org/assets/files/aga_2008_sos.pdf
8. Harrah's Entertainment Responsible Gaming. Retrieved June 18, 2008, from http://www.harrahs.com/harrahs-corporate/about-us-responsible-gaming.html
9. American Gaming Association: Responsible Gaming: History. Retrieved June 18, 2008, from http://www.americangaming.org/programs/responsiblegaming/history.cfm
10. Penn National Gaming, Inc. Retrieved June 18, 2008, from http://www.pngaming.com/main/respgaming.shtml

CHAPTER 11

THE CASINO AS A COMMUNITY NEIGHBOR

CHRIS ROBERTS

Learning Objectives

1. To provide an overview of how a casino functions as a community neighbor
2. To learn the many positive contributions that a casino has to the community
3. To learn the negative contributions that a casino has to the community
4. To learn the solutions that a casino can implement for the community

Chapter Outline

Introduction

The Positive Contributions to the Community

The Negative Contributions to the Community

Solutions That a Casino Can Implement

Conclusion

INTRODUCTION

The presence of a casino in a community changes things—in ways that are often unforeseen. As a member of the business community, the casino is an employer, a taxpayer, and a draw for business from which other businesses benefit. As an anchor tenant representing the casino industry, the business brings other types of businesses that support the casino. For example, more hospitality businesses open, bringing more lodging and restaurants to the vicinity. Dealer schools open that focus upon training new dealers. Souvenir shops open to serve tourists as do shopping and entertainment businesses. In general, the opening of a casino often brings with it a slew of different businesses that help the local community grow (Figure 11.1).

THE POSITIVE CONTRIBUTIONS TO THE COMMUNITY

There are a number of positive contributions that a casino can bring to a community. The most obvious and most often cited for casino development are the economic ones: taxes and employment. The casino business itself becomes a new taxpayer that helps to support the community. These taxes come in many forms. State and local income taxes are paid on the profits earned. Licensing of the casino and licensing of individuals who work in the casino also generate revenue for the state. The casino creates many new jobs that result in payroll taxes. Sales tax revenue is another tax that the casino helps to generate through the direct sale of food, beverages, and hotel rooms. In many states, there is an additional tax that applies to the sale of hotel rooms. In those locations, the casino helps to increase the hotel tax revenue, too. Indirect increases in sales taxes contribute to the local economy, too. The businesses that grow up around the casino or as a result of increased visitor traffic generate new sales, payroll, and income taxes, as well.

FIGURE 11.1   The famous Las Vegas Strip at night showing large signage that is brightly lit. Many other businesses have opened next to the casinos.

Source: Gunnar Kullenberg/Stock Connection.

Many new **direct** and **indirect jobs** are created when a casino opens. This helps the community by providing employment opportunities. At the top level, state governments create special task forces and casino regulatory commissions to oversee the gambling industry. Then special law enforcement officers are trained and sent to oversee the daily casino operations as well as help prevent criminal activity. Many states create their own testing laboratories for new games. When casinos get approval to build, construction crews often work around the clock to get the casino opened as fast as possible. Because of the additional construction crew and the new-hire training, many people in the community need additional services. Once the casino opens, the direct jobs are those offered by the casino itself. A large number of dealers are needed for the table games. The restaurants and lodging facilities require many workers. Entertainment for the casino requires performers and staff to help run the events. Even support functions such as security, surveillance, custodial services, marketing, human resources, and accounting provide employment opportunities. Many of these jobs require higher levels of skills and/or formal education, and provide workers with good salaries (Figure 11.2).

The indirect jobs that are created are a result of the general growth experienced in the local business community when the casino opens. Since there are more people working in the area, they may need housing, which means furniture stores, grocery stores, or anything to make a house a home. Once the new employees have housing, they need drug stores, banks, and places to eat as they get settled in and begin to live in the community. As the communities grow, they need more schools, recreation, and restaurants. The new businesses that

FIGURE 11.2 The spouting volcano at the Mirage Hotel and Casino in Las Vegas, Nevada, is a noisy and bright attraction designed to lure customers and requires specialized workers to maintain.

Source: Demetrio Carrasco © Dorling Kindersley.

FIGURE 11.3 Casinos must provide ample parking for customers to avoid creating parking nightmares on city streets.

Source: Image from BigStockPhoto.com.

grow up around a casino also help to create additional jobs for the community. Many of these new positions are a result of increased business activity for existing firms because of more visitors to the community. Some other positions are the result of the opening of new businesses related to the casino. Often, new hotels and restaurants are built near the casino to help provide services to the new visitors. New convenience stores, gas stations, and souvenir shops require workers. If the casino is near an airport, the airlines that serve it could see an increase in business, too, and may provide more flights. Additional flights will require more flight crews, ground staff, ticketing agents, customer service assistance, and so on.

This increase in visitor traffic helps to build the identity of the community as a tourist destination. Other attractions in the area can become better known as more people come to the town. As the tourism identity of the community grows, it can attract more businesses that offer other services such as live theater, museums, theme park attractions, and so on. In general, then, the opening of a casino increases visitor traffic and tourism, stimulates the local economy through job creation and increased business activity, pays a wide range of state and local taxes, and helps build market awareness of the community (Figure 11.3).

THE NEGATIVE CONTRIBUTIONS TO THE COMMUNITY

However, as tourism prospers, it also brings some negative effects. The casino owners are aware that gaining acceptance in the community is often a long and patient process. Many neighbors do not understand the role of the casino and how their community might change. Mostly, these existing neighbors initially react with fear and doubt about the benefits the casino will bring. Old clichés such as mob ownership, swarms of criminals and addicted gamblers walking the streets, and the corrupting of minors dominate many conversations.

The general perception of a casino is often negative to a community when it is first introduced. Smoke-filled rooms with many card players shouting out as they win or lose is an image that many people still carry today. Right or wrong, this is often the impression expressed in public discussions. The casino owners and senior management must work continually to dispel these myths and misimpressions.

The prevalence of crime is another frequent topic of community discussion. Historically, crime does increase in a community when a casino opens, but so does the overall **visitor count**. The percentage of new visitors in the area typically increases at a much greater rate than does the increase in crime. It is important to remember that crime increases as population density increases. For example, a town with 100 residents has a lower crime rate than New York City with its millions of residents. While the crime rate does decrease within a few years as police and the courts learn how to handle the change in the community, the crime rate doesn't return to the level existing before the casino opening. However, the total visitor count to the area doesn't return to pre-casino levels, either. This is a multiyear adjustment period. Communities do adjust, but it is often a slow and long learning process because the town is growing.

Traffic patterns shift, too. The new visitors to the community add more cars on the local roads, plus more delivery trucks and service vehicles. The resulting increase in traffic places unanticipated stress on the community highways. When added to the regular commuter traffic and weekend pleasure driving, congested roads are often a result.

With the increase in road use, the community frequently needs wider highways or perhaps new roads. The cost of these improvements, which are quite often funded by tax revenues from the casinos, falls upon the entire community and/or state. Since most communities don't have highway development funds on reserve, many times a tax increase or bond issuance is necessary. Of course, members of the community—both residential and business—share the burden of these tax increases.

More street lighting and traffic signals are also often needed to help handle the increase in traffic. Street lighting is needed to better illuminate the city streets since many casino customers gamble late into the evening and night. The traffic signals are needed to help regulate the increase in vehicles on the road. Further, more parking is needed to accommodate the additional cars and trucks in the community. While many businesses provide parking spaces at their storefront locations, as does the casino, the increase in visitors sometimes is greater than the available parking capacity. A common result is that the community must provide more parking to help deal with the issue (Figure 11.4).

Signage lighting for the casino can have a negative impact upon a community. Bright and large signage is often desired by the casino so as to attract gamblers. It helps to create an atmosphere of fun and energy. And since the casino is open all night (or late into the night, whichever is permitted by law), this bright light may be considered as **light pollution** by neighbors. Often, the signage lighting blinks, moves, or is animated in some fashion. The repetitive movement of the light is also bothersome to some (Figure 11.5).

As an entertainment facility, the casino attracts players in the evening and long into the night. The coming and going of vehicles and people generates noise. The starting and stopping of car engines can be heard for some distance. Small groups of people walking to

FIGURE 11.4 Many neighborhood streets are upgraded with lighting and other improvements to accommodate the increase in traffic and parking needs.

Source: Image from BigStockPhoto.com.

and from the casino often talk and laugh as they travel from their vehicles to the casino building. They also drive on the town streets much later in the night than was true before the casino opened. Customers may stop at gas stations to get fuel or convenience stores to pick up snacks or beverages. This constant stream of movement and noise helps create undesirable **noise pollution** for the community.

The proximity of a casino to schools and churches is often of high concern to community citizens. Typically, town regulations restrict the distance some types of business, such as liquor

FIGURE 11.5 Bright lighting around a casino helps to improve safety but can create light pollution for neighbors.

Source: Image from BigStockPhoto.com.

stores, can be from locales frequented by children. Casino locations are usually restricted in the same manner. Still, the presence of a casino in a community can be very attractive to minors. Because their emotional maturity is still developing, minors (people under 21) are often not yet capable of making good decisions about gambling. That age group does not generally have many funds, either. The lure of gambling to gain more money can be very seductive. Therefore, keeping minors out of a casino where they might create problems for themselves is of great concern to the community. The casino is expected (and required by law) to block minors from entering gaming play areas, and to immediately remove them if found gambling.

SOLUTIONS THAT A CASINO CAN IMPLEMENT

As a good neighbor in the community, there are a number of steps the casino can take to help deal with many of these new problems. As the casino is being planned, the designers can work with the local city planners to help anticipate impacts upon roads and traffic flows. If significant impacts are identified and new construction is needed, the casino and town can negotiate how much of the financial cost will be shared directly by the casino. This helps to demonstrate the casino is a good community citizen by planning ahead, and by not placing the full financial burden for the improvements upon the taxpayers.

The city planners can also work with the casino to help plan for lighting and noise issues. By submitting signage designs in advance, the planners and the casino management can work out agreeable solutions that could meet the marketing needs of the casino while balancing them with the needs of the residents (Figure 11.6). Street lighting can be added

FIGURE 11.6 The community could consider extremely large and distinctive signs as eyesores.

that anticipates the increased foot traffic so that safety is enhanced. Buffers to abate noise, such as solid walls around parking areas or the strategic placement of entrances and exits to parking lots, may help. Even the rezoning of some areas of the community can help guide the business development as growth occurs. In addition, many casinos are set apart from residential areas because they need space for the casino and for the surrounding parking. They may need more space for their resort operations like hotels, restaurants, and recreation/ entertainment complexes. They can be constructed only in specific zones so that their neighbors are other businesses. As a result, most casinos are set outside the city limits where all these effects are minimized.

Education of local law enforcement can help the community deal with anticipated increases in crime. The casino can call upon industry experts and experienced casino managers to collaborate with the local police to discuss what has happened in other communities, and to help plan for the future. Creating awareness campaigns may help other local businesses and residents understand what might happen and how they might help law enforcement deal with the situation. Such cooperation helps to build positive relationships rather than adversarial ones. People always appreciate knowing in advance what to expect and to learn how to prepare to deal with change.

Having the casino become proactive in that educational effort is a key aspect of the successful integration of the casino into the local business community. In Kenner, Louisiana, the local casino donated funds to help the police buy better equipment like computers for squad cars and more efficient communication systems so that the police could be more effective in their jobs. In addition, the casino security force asks winning gamblers if they would like an escort to their home to keep them safe. Creating an environment where criminals know it will be very difficult to prey on gamblers acts as a deterrent. It makes criminals think twice just like in the casino itself.

Public awareness campaigns regarding both minors and addictive gamblers are other contributions the casino can make to the community. Demonstrating its forethought and concern for these groups helps show the community that the casino cares about what happens to its customers and neighbors. While such campaigns are direct expenses for the casino, the investment in the local community often generates goodwill that can pay benefits later when issues may arise. A perception of the casino as a proactive partner in the community is a much more positive position from which to deal with concerns than having to constantly prod and cajole community leaders. Like most businesses, casinos need to be good neighbors. Often casinos donate funds for civic improvements like parks, playgrounds, and computers for schools. Giving back to the community is an important program.

Conclusion

The introduction of a casino into a community does create noticeable changes. These changes are both positive and negative. More than most businesses, the casino has both direct and indirect consequences for the community. The largest positive impacts are the increases in visitor traffic and tourism identity, the creation of new jobs and taxes, and the spread of new businesses around the casino location. The greatest negative impacts are the expenses of new highways and vehicle traffic, increases in crime and addiction, and the light and noise pollution that are generated. Casinos need to keep the lines of communication open so that they can quickly identify any negative effects they are creating. This will allow them to strategize the most effective way to work with the community to overcome problems. By being a proactive member of the community through involvement with town planners, local law enforcement, city officials, and educational institutions, the casino can help to make a significant impact that is both positive and helpful, and create productive relationships for years to come.

Key Words

Direct jobs *125*
Indirect jobs *125*
Visitor count *127*

Traffic patterns *127*
Signage *127*

Light pollution *127*
Noise pollution *128*

Review Questions

1. Write an overview of how a casino functions as a community neighbor.
2. Discuss the many positive contributions that a casino makes to the community.
3. Discuss the negative contributions that a casino makes to the community.
4. Explain the solutions that a casino can implement to solve problems in the community.

INDEX